DS   Abdallah, Maureen
44   Smallwood
.A25
1981   The Middle East

DATE DUE			
AUG 18 1983			
16. 20 '84			
DEC 2 0 '91			
FEB 2 2 '93			
AUG 16 1993			

The Middle East

Editor
John Liebmann
Design
Brian Paine
Picture research
Jenny Golden
Production
Rosemary Bishop
Illustrations
Hayward Art Group
Endpaper and reference maps
Matthews and Taylor Associates

Cover picture taken at the camel races at Abu Dhabi, by Christine Osborne.

Endpaper: Early morning on the bank of the Nile at Luxor.

Page 6: Traffic jams the streets of Mecca as pilgrims pray inside the Great Mosque.

First published 1980
Macdonald Educational Ltd.,
Holywell House, Worship Street
London EC2A 2EN
© Macdonald Educational 1980

Adapted and published
in the United States
by Silver Burdett Company,
Morristown, N.J.
1981 Printing

ISBN 0-382-06417-8
Library of Congress
Catalog Card No. 80-53900

The Middle East

by
Maureen Smallwood Abdallah

Silver Burdett Company

Contents

Between East and West

Spanning Africa and Asia

Fifteen countries make up the area of south-west Asia and north-west Africa we call the Middle East. Together they cover about 6.7 million square kilometres, between the Mediterranean Sea to the west and the Arabian Sea to the south-east.

At the centre of the area is the Arabian peninsula which lies between the Red Sea and the Arabian Gulf (which is also known as the Persian Gulf). Saudi Arabia occupies most of the interior. The United Arab Emirates (UAE), Qatar and Kuwait lie along the Gulf coast, while North and South Yemen and Oman line the coasts to the south. Human activity is concentrated along the coasts. To the north lie Syria, Iraq, Jordan and Lebanon. Iran, to the north-east, borders the Caspian Sea. Egypt, to the west, spans two continents: most of it lies in Africa, with only the Sinai peninsula in Asia. Much of the area known as Palestine, which borders the eastern Mediterranean, now forms part of the state of Israel.

An inhospitable climate

The countries range in size from the gigantic Saudi Arabia, which is the fourth largest country in Asia, to the tiny island state of Bahrain. The United Arab Emirates is made up of seven small sheikhdoms, the most important of which are Abu Dhabi and Dubai.

The climate can be extremely hot by day. In the deserts of the Arabian peninsula, summer temperatures soar well above 40° centigrade, though in the winter months a pleasant 15° is normal. At night the temperature often drops well below freezing. The deserts are dry, but the heat of the day along the Arabian coasts is made even more unbearable by the high humidity.

100 million people

The total population of the Middle East is well over 100 million. Most of the people are Muslims – that is, they follow the Islamic religion. In many of the countries there are Christian and Jewish minorities too. Israel is the exception, having been established in 1948 as a homeland for Jews from all over the world. The Palestinian Arabs who lived in the area before the Jewish state was set up are now a minority in Israel.

The people have a wide variety of lifestyles. The cosmopolitan city-dwellers of Beirut or Cairo have much in common with their counterparts in New York or Paris. Their lives contrast sharply with those of the tough bedouin people of the Arabian peninsula or the mountain people of Iran and Iraq.

The Middle East

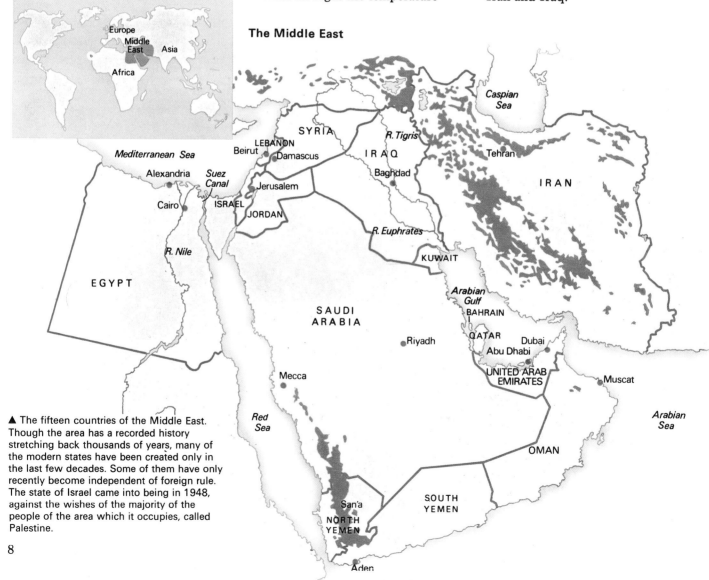

▲ The fifteen countries of the Middle East. Though the area has a recorded history stretching back thousands of years, many of the modern states have been created only in the last few decades. Some of them have only recently become independent of foreign rule. The state of Israel came into being in 1948, against the wishes of the majority of the people of the area which it occupies, called Palestine.

▲ Barren desert covers most of Egypt and Jordan, the Arabian peninsula, southern Syria and Iraq, and eastern Iran. This is the Negev desert in southern Israel. Though the desert seems to offer few rewards, it is the home of the nomadic bedouin people. Even today, when there are opportunities to settle and work in the growing cities, many bedouin prefer to continue their traditional harsh existence.

▶ The mountains of North Yemen and south-west Saudi Arabia are among the few areas in the Middle East where farming is possible. Terraces, such as these near Yarim in Yemen, allow crops to be grown on the steep mountain-side. Elsewhere, communities of mountain people live secluded independent lives.

◀ The great River Nile. The waters of the Tigris and Euphrates of Iraq and Syria, the Nile in Egypt, the Jordan, and the Orontes and Litani in Lebanon, are all vital in an area where the climate is hot and dry. What little rainfall there is usually comes during the short winter season. The rivers have traditionally been the main source of water for crop irrigation. The earliest settlers made their homes near the river banks where they built irrigation systems and water-collecting devices. Today the role of the rivers is more important than ever. The flow of water is controlled by impressive, modern dams which also generate hydro-electric power for industrial and domestic use.

▶ The elegant lines of feluccas are a common sight along the Nile. The seafaring tradition of the Middle East stretches back to the Phoenicians of the fifth and sixth centuries B.C. They sailed from the coast of what is now Lebanon and Syria to reach the west coast of Africa and beyond. In the Gulf, fishing and pearl-diving were major industries before the discovery of oil. The traditional vessels of that area, known as dhows, are larger than the feluccas. They are widely used for coastal transport and still bring in valuable cargoes of fish and shrimp.

Traditional lifestyles

Nomads of the desert

Industries are developing rapidly in the Middle East. Many people are leaving their homes in the country in the hope of finding work in the towns. But there are many others who still cling to the old way of life.

For some of the people of Egypt and Arabia, the traditional way of life is nomadic. All the governments in the Middle East have at some stage made it their official policy to encourage the nomads to settle. Although thousands have agreed to do so, many others have resisted.

In Jordan, Syria, Iran, Israel and the Arabian peninsula, there are still many people who roam the deserts with their herds in search of forage. They are increasingly replacing their camels with herds of sheep and goats and are using motorized transport for themselves and their herds. These nomads, known as bedouin, have never really acknowledged the restrictions of national boundaries.

This has always been a source of trouble between them and the authorities. They have been accused of smuggling and spreading disease. It used to be thought that their animals over-grazed the land, leaving it bare and turning good land into desert. In fact, the bedouin have been aware of the problems of over-grazing since ancient times and have learned to use even the poorest land to its best advantage, without damaging it. Now some governments are re-considering their policy. In the future the bedouin may well be encouraged to retain their old lifestyle.

Farming families

Among the settled farming people, governments have tried to introduce the idea of co-operative farming. This has usually failed. Agricultural work normally involves the whole family. Children work on the land before and after school. Women are expected to perform household tasks, as well as farm work. It is a hard existence.

Some of the farming methods are very outdated, and the prices which produce fetches are often barely enough to keep the family going. New methods cost money and are often viewed with deep suspicion, so it will take a long time for things to improve.

▼ An American pick-up has replaced camels as the means of transport for this bedouin family in Saudi Arabia. Recently many bedouin have become motorized. Several families may pool their resources to buy a truck which is used to transport both themselves and their flocks from pasture to pasture. This has the benefit of getting the animals to the short-lived forage more quickly. Just as importantly, the bedouin can now choose when to sell their animals according to demand, and can arrive at the market at the right moment and with much healthier animals.

▶ These unusual pointed dwellings and grain silos near Aleppo, in northern Syria, are built in a way that has remained unchanged for centuries. It is known that houses were being built in the Middle East around 9,000 years ago. The earliest were primitive mounds, but later mud bricks were used. Over the years they became more sophisticated, even being built on two storeys. Sometimes the bricks were left unbaked, as in southern Iraq. Elsewhere they were mixed with straw and baked, as in Egypt.

▶ Bedouin women in front of their home in Qatar. The traditional bedouin black tents have changed little in design and concept over the centuries. They are made from woven strips of goat or camel hair, each about 60 centimetres wide and anywhere between 1½ and 4 metres long. The strips are stitched together to form the main body of the tent, which is often very large. It is supported by three to five central poles, with a number of smaller poles for the sides. The tent is warm and waterproof in winter. In summer, with the side flaps raised for ventilation, it provides protection from the fierce sun. Inside there are other strips sewn together to provide walls known as *qata*. There is always one large room with a fireplace scooped out of the floor. Here the men often sit together round a charcoal fire, talking and brewing coffee. The women usually keep to the smaller rooms and look after the family while the men meet. There is no furniture, only brightly coloured woven rugs and cushions. When not in use, these are stacked to one side with the bedding, quilts and pillows.

▶ A water-buffalo provides the power to operate this old-fashioned mechanical pump, which supplies water to irrigate the field. Though some of the parts are now made of metal, wooden pumps of the same basic design have been used in Egypt for thousands of years. The animal is blindfolded so that it does not become dizzy as it plods round its circular path. Mechanized or electric water pumps are much more efficient, but most farmers are too poor to buy and install them. Other traditional agricultural techniques also survive in many parts of the Middle East. Today's hand-made wooden tools look just like those in ancient wall drawings. It is still common to see farmers, wearing the flowing blue *gallabeya*, behind a pair of oxen pulling a wooden plough of ancient design.

11

Oil and industry

Wealth from oil

Oil was discovered in the Middle East during the early decades of the twentieth century. The first major explorations did not take place until the beginning of the 1930s. One by one Saudi Arabia, Iraq, Iran, Kuwait, Qatar and The United Arab Emirates granted exploration and concession rights to the various foreign oil companies. The first oil was exported around 1934–5.

Production was stepped up after the Second World War. At this time the oil companies held almost total control of oil production, and kept a sizeable proportion of the profits. This situation continued until the early 1960s. Iraq was the first country to put a stop to this exploitation in 1961. With a dramatic move known as Law 80, it seized control of its oil reserves and nationalized the industry.

Other states eventually followed suit but it was not until the late 1970s that all the major producers took control of the industries which extracted their oil resources.

Diversification

The growth of the oil industry has completely changed the areas where oil is produced. It transformed a backward, unproductive desert of little value into one of the wealthiest regions in the world.

Nobody knows the true extent of the oil reserves, but it is certain that one day the oil will run out. The oil producers themselves are acutely conscious of this fact, and they are already taking steps to diversify their growing economies away from oil and into other fields. They hope that their countries will soon become thriving industrial producers.

In late 1973 the price of oil increased four-fold overnight. It has gone up several times since. This sudden increase brought billions of dollars flooding into the producing countries. The governments concerned had to act quickly to channel this money into productive areas. A new banking and investment sector was created.

Kuwait has a tiny population and produces large quantities of oil. It therefore has one of the highest per capita incomes in the world. Some others, by contrast, have very little oil and a large population. These less fortunate countries must continually borrow to keep their economies going.

Developing new industries

Besides investing their surplus cash, the oil-producing countries also decided to use some of their oil in new industries of their own. Petrochemical production is one such industry, which uses the oil as a starting material to make various valuable chemicals.

In Saudi Arabia comprehensive industrial complexes are being built at

◀ Oil wells in the Qatar desert, with surplus gas burning off in huge flares. Though they are undeniably spectacular, these flares are a waste of a precious resource. Increasingly, the gases produced with petroleum are being used locally as fuel or are compressed and exported.

▶ Mercedes trucks being assembled in Saudi Arabia. Assembly plants for cars and domestic appliances are now being set up in the Middle East to supply local markets. Eventually these may be replaced by locally based industries making consumer products from scratch.

Jubail on the Gulf coast and Yenbo on the Red Sea. When completed, these will include steel mills and aluminium factories as well as petrochemical and other oil-related industries. This heavy investment has led to the development of other fields such as the construction industry and the transport sector.

Mouths to feed

Countries like Egypt and Syria have very little oil. Jordan and Lebanon have none at all. They have concentrated more on building up their traditional agricultural industry. They are among the most highly populated countries, and in Egypt and Syria the cost of feeding the rapidly growing population is a major strain on the economy.

Throughout the area there is a shortage of skilled workers. For decades Egypt, Jordan, Lebanon and the Palestinians have been the main source of trained labour for the entire area. Now there is a major drive among the oil-producing states to train more skilled workers for all sectors of industry. Meanwhile, in the oil-producing states, top management posts are still largely filled by Western professionals. A large portion of the unskilled and semi-skilled work is carried out by immigrant workers from Asia.

▲ In some ways oil is much too precious to be simply burned. It contains (or can be converted into) chemical compounds which cannot be conveniently produced any other way. This plant in Qatar uses local oil to produce the fertilizer needed by the developing local agricultural industry.

▼ In contrast to the new industries based on oil and the wealth derived from it, Egypt and Syria have a textile industry dating back hundreds of years. This Egyptian textile mill was built as part of a programme of investment in modern machinery to spin and weave cotton. Whether this investment will go much further, or whether the land will eventually be turned over to food instead of cotton production is a subject under discussion.

City life

Bursting at the seams

In the older cities the effect of the sudden influx of people from the countryside has been disastrous. Most have not been able to cope with the huge volume of traffic and people. They have neither the housing facilities nor the basic services to provide for the needs of their inhabitants. As a result there has been severe strain at all levels, and some city areas are now slums. Families moved to the city in the hope of making good money. Instead, many find themselves living in dire poverty, several to a room, short of water, electricity and even food.

In the modern cities of the Gulf, space is more abundant and there is more room for development. But even here there are housing problems and shortages. The money available from oil production has led to rapid growth, and there has not been enough time to establish adequate services for the new population. The booming economies of the Gulf states have attracted thousands of immigrant labourers, especially from Asia. They cannot afford the high rents which are charged, so they too are reduced to living in poor conditions, many to a room.

The rush to modernize

In the Gulf the pace of modernization has been very rapid indeed. Buildings have often been thrown together haphazardly with little thought for practicality or design. In the space of a few years the bare desert has become filled with towering skyscrapers or straggling residential complexes.

Few people gave much thought to town planning. Quickness and convenience were the aim, and the results were usually ugly and shabby. Sadly, a lot of beautiful old buildings have been destroyed and replaced by huge, characterless office blocks. In many cities speculation in office buildings and blocks of flats has run wild. Buildings which were erected in the hope of big profits have stayed empty for years because the rents are too high or the demand for office space too low.

Some areas have a strange mixture of styles. In the residential district of Kuwait City, rich home owners can afford to indulge in their dream houses. Here, buildings resembling the Washington White House, a New England mansion and a Chinese pagoda all stand within a few hundred metres of each other.

Refugees

A number of cities have suffered additional strains from refugees flocking in from troubled areas. Cairo now houses many people from around Suez. Troubles in southern Lebanon have caused many to flee to Beirut, and Amman is now the home of thousands of Palestinians who fled from the Israeli-occupied West Bank of Jordan.

▶ The back streets of Cairo, Egypt's capital city. Originally founded a thousand years ago as a spacious city on the Nile delta, it later had very little room in which to grow. Now it is struggling, with a population of nine million. Every year the problem gets worse as the population increases. Cairo is a city literally bursting at the seams. The streets are always crowded. The pavements, where they exist at all, are cracked and broken. The roads are jammed with heavy traffic. Many buildings are in such a state of disrepair that they are literally crumbling with age and neglect. Everything is in short supply. Only in the exclusive residential areas, or by the river at night, can the beauty that was once Cairo be glimpsed again.

◀ The old market area of *souq* of the Iranian city of Esfahan. Though the city is now an industrial centre with numerous modern textile factories, the flourishing *souq* survives in the centre of the old city. The *souq* is still a feature of many Middle Eastern cities, where life appears to have changed little over the centuries. Almost everything can be bought, from sheepskins to sugar, jugs to jewellery, pipes to pomegranates. One of the finest examples in the area is the *souq* at Aleppo, Syria, which stretches for over 15 kilometres.

◀ San'a, capital of North Yemen. Many of the ancient cities of the Middle East have suffered disastrously from unplanned development. The marvellous city of San'a is one of the few to have remained intact. It is world famous for its multi-storey stone houses built on huge rock foundations, towering high over the narrow streets. Following the first unsuccessful attempts to modernize, the authorities of San'a are trying to come up with plans which allow the city to grow within the style and character of the oldest parts.

▶ The new *'supersouqs'* of the Gulf are a startling contrast to the old-fashioned markets of the surrounding area. These giant, Western-style supermarkets have suddenly appeared. They sell goods from all over the world: New Zealand ice-cream, English apples and gourmet French cheeses, as well as every imaginable sort of packed or canned food. There is no more haggling, no more bargaining over the price of goods. Instead, shopping is quick, easy and impersonal. Perhaps some people regret the passing of the old ways, but overall the experiment is welcomed.

Ancient civilizations

The first settlements

In about 7000 B.C. the first people ever to build their own homes were settling in the area of Mesopotamia, which is now southern Iraq. The Sumerians, who settled the same area around 5000 B.C., are the first civilization of which we have a comprehensive knowledge, but it seems that a thriving culture had already been at work before them. The potter's wheel had already been invented, and the people were following an established religion which included the worship of various symbolic gods.

The Sumerians built the city of Ur on a strategic site near the mouth of the Euphrates river. Ur developed into a thriving centre for trade between the Indian Ocean and the Mediterranean.

Invasion follows invasion

The Sumerians were replaced by a succession of new invaders. The first of these were the Amorites who founded the kingdom of Babylon. King Hammurabi, who lived from 1792 to 1750 B.C., has the distinction of being the first ruler to devise and record a comprehensive system of rules and laws. These governed such things as the sale of water rights, land, and cattle, and regulated the maintenance of canals and the conduct of business.

At around the same time, the area to the north-west (which now forms part of Syria, Lebanon and Israel) was occupied by the people known in the Bible as the Canaanites. They were followed by the Phoenicians. It was there that the basis of today's alphabet was developed.

By 1466 B.C. an Indo-European people called the Hittites had occupied Syria and Iraq and were ruling over the whole area. As the Hittite empire declined, around 1200 B.C., their place was taken by the Assyrians, who remained in power for almost 600 years. They became the first outsiders to invade Egypt, getting as far as the city of Memphis.

In 631 B.C. the Assyrians were ousted by the Neo-Babylonians. They proved to be clever at business as well as skilled in crafts and tough fighters. They set up a banking system and conducted a profitable export business in dates, wheat and wool. When the Egyptians tried to interfere in Syria and Palestine, the Neo-Babylonians strengthened their grip by invading

Jerusalem on two occasions.

By 539 B.C. the might of the Persians of the Achaemenid empire to the north was growing. By 530 B.C. they had conquered Babylon and Syria, and that year they went on to conquer Egypt. At its height the empire stretched as far as Greece.

Foreign rulers

The Achaemenid empire came to an end in 331 B.C. when the armies of Darius III were defeated by invaders from the Greek kingdom of Macedon. The Macedonians, led by Alexander the Great, quickly established control over the whole of the Middle East. From then on the area remained under foreign rule for many centuries.

After the death of Alexander in 323 B.C., the Macedonian empire was divided several times and ruled by various Greek dynasties until the Romans arrived in 188 B.C. They waged a bitter fight for the area, but never gained control of Persia and Babylon. They were continually troubled by local unrest, and in the fourth century A.D. rule from Rome eventually gave way to rule from the Byzantine capital Constantinople.

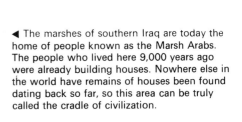

◀ The marshes of southern Iraq are today the home of people known as the Marsh Arabs. The people who lived here 9,000 years ago were already building houses. Nowhere else in the world have remains of houses been found dating back so far, so this area can be truly called the cradle of civilization.

Remains of the city of Persepolis still stand in the mountains of south-western Iran. Persepolis was founded in 521 B.C. It was developed by the Achaemenid rulers Darius and Xerxes as one of the capitals of their empire. In its time the Achaemenid or Persian empire was the largest the Middle East had ever seen. Under the leadership of Cyrus the Great it spread out from Iran, sweeping through Babylon to Syria. After Cyrus's death in 530 B.C. the Achaemenids went on to conquer Egypt, under the leadership of Cyrus's son Cambyses. They later extended their empire as far as Greece. Under the command of Xerxes their armies even managed to capture Athens and hold it for a short time. The Achaemenid rulers maintained overall control while allowing each kingdom to keep its own institutions, language and customs. The empire was divided into regions known as *satrapies*. Each one was governed by a governor, a general and a secretary of state chosen by the emperor. Power was divided between them and all three reported directly to the king. The provinces were taxed according to their resources and there was a highly developed system of book-keeping. The king's inspectors travelled the empire on roads which were specially built for that purpose, though they were used by traders too. There was a well-disciplined garrison in every area so that if revolt did break out it was quickly crushed. Much of Persepolis was destroyed when the empire was overrun by the Macedonian armies of Alexander the Great, yet even today its magnificence is obvious. The relief work which decorates the walls is of the highest quality. It contains a great deal of information about the state of the empire and its history, its affluence and importance.

▶ Roman remains at Jerash, just north of the present-day Jordanian capital of Amman. Wherever they spread their empire the Romans built magnificent towns, temples and palaces. One of their purposes was to assert Roman wealth and power by their sheer grandeur. Jerash was a flourishing Roman town for many hundreds of years, and reached its peak in the third century A.D. It boasted two amphitheatres, a beautiful temple dedicated to the goddess Artemis, and a triumphal arch dedicated to the emperor Hadrian.

◀ The people of ancient Egypt built huge monuments to their rulers. These are the Colossi of Memnon which stand in the desert near Luxor. While various groups were fighting for supremacy in the areas of Iraq, Syria and Palestine, Egypt enjoyed a period of stability and prosperity. Around 3,000 B.C. King Menes of Upper Egypt united his kingdom with Lower Egypt. The kings, or pharaohs, ruled Egypt for over 2,000 years. Under their rule there was an efficient system of administration and taxation run by a central government. The kingdom was supported by a flourishing agricultural system and defended by a strong army. The arts developed, together with a unique architectural style. Among the surviving monuments of ancient Egypt are the pyramids near Cairo, the magnificent temples of Upper Egypt and the obelisks which now stand in Paris and London.

Three world religions

▶ The Royal Mosque at Esfahan, Iran, one of the great Shia mosques. When Mohammed died a bitter dispute broke out over who should lead the Muslims. The first four leaders, known as caliphs, were chosen from the Prophet's immediate family. The fourth one, Ali, was appointed in 656, but his rule was seriously challenged by members of the Ummayyad people in Syria. When Ali was assassinated in 661, the Ummayyads seized power, and for the first time the Muslims were divided. Those who followed Ali and his descendants became known as Shia Muslims. The rest fell in line with the Ummayyads and became known as Sunni (orthodox) Muslims. Today the Sunnis form the majority of Muslims generally, except in Iran and Iraq, where the Shias have the majority. Though the two branches of the faith subscribe to the basic tenets of Islam, they sometimes differ widely in their interpretation of the Koran and in some of their religious ceremonies.

▼ A chapel in Jerusalem belonging to the Coptic Christian church.

Jewish history

The history of the Jews, which was acted out in the lands of the Middle East, is inseparably bound up with the traditions and customs of the Jewish religion today. The first great Temple was built in Jerusalem nearly 3,000 years ago, though it was later destroyed by invaders. The Western Wall of the second Temple, which was itself built before 500 B.C., still stands today and is the holiest shrine of Judaism.

Though many Jews left the Middle East to settle in other parts of the world, some stayed behind. Even today there are still Jewish communities living and worshipping in many parts of the Middle East.

Birthplace of Christ

The Middle East is also the focus of the Christian religion. Bethlehem, Christ's birthplace, is just a few kilometres south of Jerusalem in the area that is now the Israeli-occupied West Bank. Christ was crucified in Jerusalem itself. Bethlehem and Jerusalem attract Christian pilgrims from all over the world, especially at Christmas and Easter.

Many of the people of the Middle East today are Christians. The Coptic Christians of Egypt comprise one in ten of the country's population. In Lebanon, the Maronites are an important political and religious force.

Their sect derives from the order of monks founded in the sixth century by St Maron, a Syrian priest. Among the many other Christian denominations active in the Middle East are Roman Catholics, Greek Catholics, Protestants and Armenian Christians.

Centre of Islam

Mohammed, the founder of Islam, was a member of the semi-nomadic people called the Quraysh who lived around Mecca, in what is now Saudi Arabia. He was said to have been an honest and reasonably successful trader. He was also, it seems, a contemplative man who was deeply concerned about the material and moral welfare of his people.

Mohammed was over 40 when he experienced a revelation from Allah. At this time Christianity was about 600 years old and Judaism had been established for about 2,000 years. The Arabs did not follow either religion, and were still not committed to the idea of one God. The Jews and Christians tended to look down on the Arabs as infidels.

It was against this background that Mohammed received his first visitation from the Angel Gabriel. He was in retreat on the hillsides outside Mecca when the word of God was revealed to him. At first Mohammed was terrified by what had happened, but the visions continued. After a great deal of questioning and self-doubt he began to preach in 613.

The ruling authorities were disturbed by Mohammed's new movement since it rejected many aspects of their pleasure-loving lives. In 622 their opposition forced Mohammed to leave Mecca. This departure became known as *Hijra* (which means migration). It marks the beginning of the Muslim calendar.

Mohammed eventually settled in Medina. It was here that Islam (which means submission) became an organized religious force. Over the years he increased his authority and his following. When war eventually broke out between Mecca and Medina, Mohammed and his followers were able to conquer Mecca in 630.

During this time Mohammed had instructed the people on the ideas and laws revealed to him by God. These were copied down by friends and followers. After Mohammed's death they were collected together in the Muslim holy book, the Koran.

▲ Jerusalem, the holy city. Judaism, Christianity and Islam all have important shrines within Jerusalem, and the city is unique in being regarded as sacred by all three religions. The golden Dome of the Rock is one of the most sacred Muslim shrines. The Dome stands on Temple Mount, site of the ancient Jewish temple. The western wall of the Temple, also known as the Wailing Wall, is still standing. It is the most sacred of all the holy places of the Jewish religion.

▼ Druse outside the temple at Baalbec in northern Lebanon. Following the great split in the Muslim faith between Shia and Sunni, other groups and sects broke away. The Druse were established at the beginning of the 11th century. They now live in small, secluded communities mainly in Lebanon and Syria. The Alawites are another minority group who practise an extreme form of Shiism. They live mainly in Syria where they are an influential minority.

The spread of Islam

The Islamic conquests
After Mohammed died in 632, his followers set out with great zeal to spread the word of Islam. Under Islamic rule the whole of the Middle East was united for the first time. There was one language and one culture. From 660 the vast empire was ruled from Damascus by the Ummayyads. In 750 they were overthrown by the Abbasids, descendants of one of Mohammed's uncles.

The Golden Age
The Abbasids moved their capital from Damascus to Baghdad in 762, and this began the Golden Age of Islam. Baghdad flourished as a centre of learning. The arts developed under the rule of Caliph Haroun al Rachid, famous for the Tales of 1001 Arabian Nights. Scholars, poets, scientists and mathematicians flocked to the court.

The Persians willingly embraced the new faith, as did many in the former Byzantine empire. Islam itself was greatly enriched by the varied cultural influences from different parts of its empire.

Division and conquest
The first wave of invaders were the Seljuk Turks. After defeating the Byzantine army in 1071, they spread their empire eastwards through Baghdad to Persia. Baghdad remained a centre of learning until 1258 when it was destroyed by Mongol invaders from central Asia.

Meanwhile, in Egypt the Ismailis had gained power. Later known as the Fatimids, they founded the city of Cairo in 969. Under the Fatimids, Cairo grew into an intellectual and spiritual centre to rival Baghdad.

Turkish influence was established in Egypt by a powerful group of mercenaries called Mamelukes. They had originally been slaves of the Arabs, and after being freed they were hired as bodyguards to protect the caliph. By 1260 they had grown so influential that they were able to take over themselves. They remained in power in Egypt until the Ottomans

from Turkey swept through the entire region and captured Cairo in 1516.

The crusades
In Europe, the forces of Christendom rose up against Islam and recaptured Spain. There then began a series of crusades to capture the Holy Land for Christianity. By 1099 Jerusalem had been captured. Vast numbers of Muslims and Jews were massacred, along with many members of rival Christian sects. The Crusaders remained in occupation until 1187, when they were defeated by the Muslim leader Salah al Din who restored Jerusalem to Muslim rule.

▶ A sixteenth-century Ottoman painting illustrating the campaign westwards. From their original territory in western Turkey, the Ottoman Turks spread their empire north-westwards into Europe and south and east to cover North Africa and most of the Arab Middle East. Only the interior of the Arabian peninsula managed to remain independent.

▼ The influence of Islam spread quickly. Arabia itself came under Muslim rule before the Prophet died. By 750 most of North Africa had been overcome, and from there influence had spread up through Spain. In 732 the Muslim invaders managed to reach Poitiers in central France before being turned back.

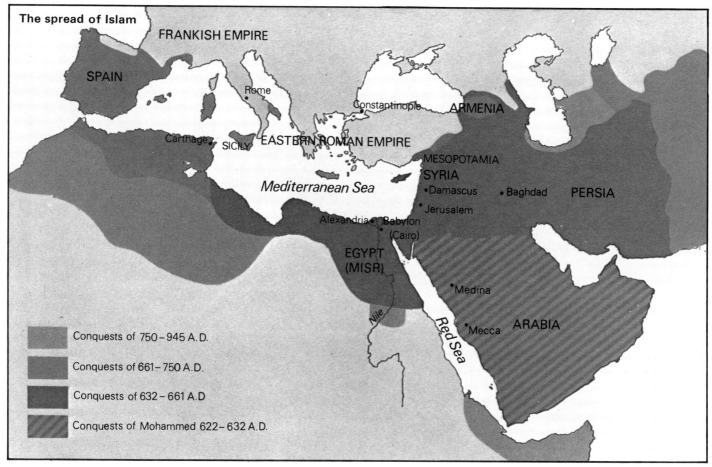

The spread of Islam

FRANKISH EMPIRE

SPAIN

Rome

Carthage

SICILY

EASTERN ROMAN EMPIRE

Constantinople

ARMENIA

Mediterranean Sea

MESOPOTAMIA

SYRIA

• Damascus

• Baghdad

PERSIA

• Jerusalem

Alexandria • Babylon (Cairo)

EGYPT (MISR)

Nile

• Medina

Red Sea

• Mecca   ARABIA

Conquests of 750–945 A.D.

Conquests of 661–750 A.D.

Conquests of 632–661 A.D

Conquests of Mohammed 622–632 A.D.

Foreign rule

Invasion from the West

In 1798 the French armies of Napoleon invaded Egypt. Napoleon's aim was to gain control of Britain's main trading routes to India. Botanists, astrologers, artists and archaeologists came in the wake of the army. Their writings about the wonders of Egypt aroused the interest of the whole of Europe.

▲ Mohammed Ali (1769–1849) challenged the supremacy of the Ottomans in Egypt and became the country's effective ruler in 1811. He was a great admirer of Napoleon and made many reforms in Egypt's education, agriculture, industry and defence. To do this he imported foreign instructors, mainly from France. Ali's descendants continued in power until the last of Egypt's monarchs, the pampered, corrupt King Farouk, was forced to abdicate in 1952.

Napoleon's invasion was a failure, and in 1800 France was forced to evacuate. But it was nevertheless an event of great significance since it alerted the British to the strategic importance of Egypt and the possible threat to their interests in India.

The brief French occupation also had an important effect on the people of Egypt who had long been subjected to the oppressive rule of the Turks. The country's élite became increasingly aware of how far they themselves had fallen behind the Western world.

Egypt breaks free

The Ottomans were seriously alarmed by the invasion. They responded with a new force which they sent into the area under the command of an able leader, an Albanian named Mohammed Ali. Ali quickly gained the confidence of the Egyptian people and he was nominated governor of Egypt in 1805. He was unpopular with the Mamelukes who had previously been allowed to rule Egypt without interference from Constantinople. In 1811 Ali engineered a massacre of the Mamelukes.

Ali used his position to make far-reaching changes inside Egypt. He also went on to extend his authority into Arabia and on to Syria, as well as southwards into Sudan. This caused considerable concern to the British, who saw their interests in the area being increasingly threatened.

A treaty signed in London by Austria, Britain, Russia and Prussia in 1841 severely curtailed Ali's ambitions. British influence in Egypt grew, and with it the gradual incursion of the other Western powers into the Middle East.

England and France became fierce rivals in Egypt, especially over the Suez Canal. They vied with each other for control of the other countries in the region in a long power struggle.

Nationalism

Meanwhile the seeds of nationalism were taking root. The first signs became apparent when the Egyptian army, led by a certain Colonel Arabi, began subscribing to the slogan 'Egypt for the Egyptians'. Arabi's movement gathered such force that the British decided to step in. They invaded in 1882 and remained in occupation for the following 70 years, with profound repercussions throughout the area.

Foreign influence in the Middle East

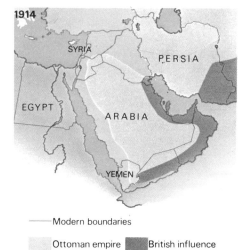

—— Modern boundaries

Ottoman empire

Russian influence

British influence

British occupation

▲ Before the outbreak of the First World War in 1914 the Ottoman empire still ruled much of the Middle East. In the west it stretched through Palestine and along the Red Sea as far as Yemen. To the east it covered Syria and part of Iraq to reach the Persian Gulf. British influence was confined to Egypt, the southern coast of Arabia, and the Gulf. Russian influence extended into the northern part of Iran. Only the barren areas of central Arabia and south-west Iran were free of direct foreign interference.

—— Modern boundaries

Turkey

British mandate areas and colonies

British/French occupation in Egypt

French mandate

▲ In 1916 the British and French governments signed the document known as the Sykes-Picot agreement. This arranged for vast areas of Arab land to be divided between spheres of influence under British and French control. It ran directly contrary to promises which were made by Britain to Hussein, the Sherif of Mecca, in return for Arab support against the Turks. The Sykes-Picot agreement formed the basis of the way territory was divided at the end of the First World War in 1918. Britain remained in control in Egypt and kept the strategically important colony at Aden. The territories of Iraq, Transjordan and Palestine also came under British influence, while the French took Syria and Lebanon.

Betrayal and struggle

Elsewhere in the region the Ottoman rulers were faced with competition from the Western powers as well as the demands of Arab nationalists. From time to time the Arabs and the West worked together against their common enemy, the Turks. During the First World War, which broke out in 1914, Western powers were fighting Germany and Turkey. In return for promises to help them in their nationalist cause, the Arabs supported the West against Turkey.

The Arabs' struggle was long and bitter. After the end of the First World War they were let down time and again by their allies. It was not until well after the end of the Second World War that foreign rule was eliminated from most of the Middle East. The effect of these betrayals is still being felt today, and the problems of the Palestinians can be traced back to these years.

Agriculture

Irrigation for farming

Centuries ago the Middle East was one of the world's main food-growing areas. From the time of the Sumerians and the Pharaohs, some 5,000 years ago, the people practised farming in the fertile river valleys of the Tigris, the Euphrates, the Nile and the Jordan. A wide variety of cereals, fruit and vegetables were grown here.

Because the area was generally arid, and rainfall was scarce, irrigation systems and water conveying devices had to be used. The collection and distribution of water soon reached sophisticated levels. In the desert areas, surface water was seldom found. But wherever there were signs of water, the people sunk wells and cut channels to allow prosperous oases to spring up.

▲ Governments throughout the Middle East are encouraging farmers to try better land management schemes, such as the planting of fruit trees. Besides giving high yields, these schemes also help prevent soil erosion. At the same time new types of greenhouses and plastic planting tunnels are being tested. These give the vegetables added protection and are proving very successful. The prize-winning cabbage shown here was grown on an experimental farm in Qatar. Extensive land reclamation and fertilization schemes are also under way in the hope that vast quantities of grain will eventually be planted.

From these early times until the 13th century, when the forces of Genghis Khan invaded, the area remained productive and prosperous. The Mongol warriors destroyed vast cultivated areas. Many irrigation systems were smashed, while others fell into disrepair. The gradual encroachment of the desert swallowed up much of the fertile land, and farming became impossible in many places. Elsewhere, for example in the Nile valley, farming continued to progress. The people of the fertile Nile delta had learned to monitor and divert the flood water.

Changing needs

The nature of agricultural production changed according to the needs of the people. Egypt under Mohammed Ali was a major producer of cotton. It was sold overseas to provide money to maintain Ali's huge army. Nowadays the Egyptian government is encouraging the production of food crops to meet the needs of Egypt's rapidly expanding population.

Throughout the Middle East, food production has high priority. The population of the region is expanding rapidly and, as food becomes scarcer all over the world, imported supplies become more expensive and less dependable. All the governments in the area are giving high priority to agriculture and to the redevelopment of some of the lost arable areas.

New methods

The farmers are exploring new methods, and increasingly ambitious irrigation systems are being built. The problems of water conservation are constantly being studied. Dams are built wherever possible to conserve water supplies and control the flow of rivers. Drainage canals are dug and swamps are drained, while the reclaimed land is liberally fertilized for new planting.

At present only an estimated 10 per cent of land in the Middle East is cultivated. Food is one of the major, most costly imports. The task of increasing local food production is enormous, but where money is available there has been no hesitation in importing and adapting the most advanced technology. The latest equipment, the newest seed types and the best fertilizers are all being tested in the effort to increase food production.

▼ In a number of countries in the Middle East, encouraging results have been obtained from hydroponic farms. In this picture, cucumbers are being grown hydroponically in a greenhouse in Abu Dhabi. This method of cultivation allows plants to be grown in plastic tubes, without soil. They are fed only by liquids. Plant food is dissolved in water which is pumped through the tubes. Crops such as tomatoes and cucumbers can often be harvested within a few weeks of planting in these tubes, which are housed in temperature-controlled greenhouses.

▲ Water is the key to successful agricultural production in the Middle East. Here cotton is growing in an irrigated field near Ashkelon in southern Israel. In order to supply the needs of agriculture, many new water conservation schemes have been initiated throughout the area. There are now dams across the Nile at Aswan, Egypt, across the Euphrates in Syria, the Tigris in Iraq, the Zerka river in Jordan and the Jizan in Saudi Arabia. Water stored in reservoirs behind the dams is released whenever it is needed, allowing for an increased number of growing seasons in most areas. The dams also provide hydro-electric power to drive new mechanized equipment. In the Gulf states elaborate water desalination plants have been built to produce fresh water from sea water, though these require huge quantities of energy to operate.

▼ Dairy farming was unheard of in the Arabian peninsula until recently. Now in Saudi Arabia and the Gulf states there are an increasing number of herds. At this experimental cattle farm near Salalah in southern Oman, high-yielding Friesian cattle are crossed with breeds which can survive in the hot climate. In this way good yields of milk can be obtained from cattle living out in the open. Elsewhere cattle are kept in environmentally controlled sheds. The floors are slatted to allow the cows' waste to fall through into underground tanks. It is then used to fertilize nearby fields where crops are grown for fodder. The cows must be quite happy in their air-conditioned homes for they produce three times the normal amount of milk. There are similar poultry farms where the chickens grow up indoors, unaffected by the fierce sun.

▲ Traditional farming methods still flourish in some areas of the Middle East. Usually agriculture depends on water from nearby rivers or from underground, but here in Asir province in south-western Saudi Arabia there is enough rainfall to water the crops. To make the most of this limited fertile area, terraces have been built in the mountain-side making usable fields on their steep slopes. In Asir province and in North Yemen there has always been a large rural population. Millet, wheat, maize and barley are grown in these areas, as well as many different kinds of fruit and vegetables ranging from bananas, citrus and dates to grapes, tomatoes, carrots and onions. One crop peculiar to the area is a shrub called *qat*. Its leaves are chewed for their intoxicating effect.

Transport and communication

Moving the freight

It was not so long ago that land transport in many parts of the Middle East meant simply camel caravans across wide expanses of desert. Sea transport was provided by beautiful sailing boats called dhows.

In an area developing as rapidly as the Middle East, however, the days of the camel and dhow are quickly becoming folklore. This is a time of rapid industrial expansion. Huge amounts of money are being spent on imported equipment and materials to supply the growing industries and expanding cities. To deal with this massive traffic, transport facilities are themselves being improved very rapidly. New airports cater for the passenger traffic while ports and roads are being built as quickly as possible to handle the goods.

This growth has been so fast in the last 50 years that the coastlines of the Middle East have been transformed. Major ports and oil terminals have been set up along the Gulf coast and the Red Sea in order to handle the constant flow of oil tankers and freighters plying these waters.

Despite this rapid growth, the ports have been unable to keep up with demand. Other outlets were needed, and suppliers turned to road transport as one way round the serious problem of port congestion. This in turn required the building of extensive new road networks.

Travel for the wealthy

Alongside all this, air transport developed. The more the Middle East flourishes, the greater the flow of air traffic. Business people travel from the West to make their oil deals and sell their goods, technology and expertise.

At the same time, the local people have become more affluent and have been exposed to Western ideas. They, in turn, have become curious to travel. The wealthier Arabs travel to the West for business or to invest their money. Some spend their holidays there or take medical treatment.

New airports have mushroomed as rapidly as the ports. Now every country or state has one, two or more. Some of them are among the most modern in the world. Every country has its own national airline. Some, like Middle East Airlines of Lebanon, have received international awards for service and dependability. Others, like the comparatively young Gulf Air, take pains to offer passengers every possible comfort in an effort to build up their reputation.

Modern telecommunications

In establishing the transport sector, many countries had enough money to invest in the latest equipment and methods. The same applies to telecommunications. Enormous contracts have been awarded to install some of the very latest telephone, television and radio equipment.

Some of the television stations are so up to date that there is a problem finding trained personnel to run them. In the age of satellite communication the Middle East has no intention of being left behind in this field. The governments have recently come to an agreement to build their own regional satellite, due to be launched in the early 1980s.

The Arabic press started to develop at the same time as Arab nationalism, first in Lebanon and later in Egypt. It is the region's strongest medium and, despite censorship problems, continues to thrive and expand.

◀ Airport buildings throughout the world have become status symbols, and Middle East countries are no exception. This is the new terminal at Abu Dhabi. An aircraft belonging to Middle East Airlines can be seen parked on the apron outside. Even the smallest states have an airport of their own, though there is sometimes not enough traffic for them all to be properly used. The airports at Sharja and Dubai, two members of the United Arab Emirates, are so close together that several pilots have landed at the wrong one by mistake. Older-established airports can have different problems. Cairo airport, for example, suffers from outdated equipment and is often overloaded.

▶ Unloading timber at Bahrain docks. New docks have been built at several points along the coast to handle imported consignments in bulk or in containers. Oil, the area's main export, is shipped from specialized terminals. There has also been a proliferation of service facilities connected with the shipping trade. These include huge dry docks projects to handle both shipbuilding and repairs, especially for the big oil tankers. The two most important ones are in Bahrain and Dubai. Though they are less costly for tankers than the European yards, they still have to compete with the cheaper docks in the Far East. There is also a shortage of skilled labour to operate them.

◀ Road transport is changing fast. Here old meets new as a Swedish-made, Saudi-owned truck passes some more traditional forms of transport on the outskirts of Jidda. For increasing numbers of European truck drivers, the once exotic names, Istanbul, Shiraz, Abu Dhabi or Kuwait, have become part of everyday working life. Nowadays drivers regularly chalk up thousands of kilometres between Europe and the Middle East, their huge trucks pounding down the motorways of Europe and across seemingly endless stretches of barren desert. They are part of a vital chain transmitting goods to this part of the world. Though it is a tough, gruelling ride, many drivers now have it worked out to the last detail. They know all the ins and outs of border formalities and custom controls, and their cabs have been adapted into what look like mini-motel rooms.

◀ A receiving station standing in the desert of Oman forms part of the country's satellite communications link with the outside world. Many nations have by-passed older methods of telecommunication and gone straight to the most modern. Up-to-date telephone equipment allows direct dialling from almost anywhere in Saudi Arabia and the Gulf to Europe, North America and the Far East.

▶ While most of the countries have managed to sort out their international communications quite efficiently, the same cannot be said about getting round and about the cities. There is very little public transport and what there is can often be inadequate. This train carries passengers to and from work in Cairo. Buses are equally overcrowded, with people crammed inside until there is no room to breathe, and more on the roof or clinging to the sides for dear life. Terrible traffic jams in the cities are made worse by erratic driving and the habit of leaning on the horn when all else fails.

The customs of Islam

A way of life

For followers of Islam, religion is a way of life. From the moment the sun rises in the morning to late at night, practising Muslims follow a daily routine of prayer and devotion, no matter where they are. Their faith is based on a system of beliefs and customs known broadly as the Five Pillars of Islam. These are belief in Allah (God), prayer, fasting, pilgrimage and giving alms.

The Muslim place of worship is called a mosque. It need be no more than a simple oblong building. But some mosques are extremely elaborate and beautiful buildings, often with a huge dome supported by hundreds of pillars. Many mosques are decorated both inside and out with intricate ceramics and stucco work. Every mosque has a tall, slender tower called a minaret. There are five times each day at which Muslims must stop what they are doing and pray. In the past a man known as a *muezzin* climbed the minaret to call the worshippers to prayer. Now the *muezzin* have been replaced by loudspeakers which are switched on at the appointed hours of prayer.

The holy day of the Muslim week is Friday. In most Middle Eastern countries the weekend starts on a Thursday afternoon and it is back to work on Saturday morning. During Friday worshippers spend a long time at the mosque either praying or listening to recitations from the Muslim holy book, the Koran. Sermons are given by the religious leaders, who are known as sheikhs.

Words of the Prophet

The Koran, together with the *hadiths* (words and sayings of the Prophet Mohammed), provide a complete guide for all aspects of life. They include guidance on marriage, divorce, child rearing, inheritance, justice and the conduct of business.

The Koran is about the same length as the New Testament of the Bible, and is divided into chapters. It is said to have been dictated directly to Mohammed from God by the Angel

▲ The Kaaba, a large rectangular container in the courtyard of the Great Mosque at Mecca. It contains a sacred black stone. Every Muslim who can possibly manage it must make a pilgrimage to Mecca at least once. Mecca is the holiest place of Islam where the Prophet Mohammed lived and spread the word of Allah. This pilgrimage, known as the *Hadj*, takes place in the twelfth lunar month of the Muslim year. It involves very special rites including the temporary renunciation of all earthly possessions, fasting, prayer and devotions. Every pilgrim entering the holy city of Mecca has to leave behind all possessions, and wears only two simple white sheets. One of the most important parts of the *Hadj* is to touch the Kaaba. In the courtyard of the Great Mosque thousands of pilgrims circle around for hours on end, slowly making their way towards the Kaaba until they are near enough to touch it.

◀ The Ummayyad Mosque at Damascus, Syria, was founded in the eighth century. It is a mosque of the Sunni sect. Though a mosque need be nothing more than a simple rectangular building, many are very fine buildings indeed.

Gabriel. The Arabic of the Koran is particularly beautiful and perfect. Mohammed could not read or write. He is said to have memorized the angel's words and dictated them to friends and followers. The Koran is a complete guide to life and devotion and all Muslims are required to read it at least once in their life.

Religious law
The legal system in Muslim countries is called *sharia* and is based on the instructions given in the Koran. The details of the law are interpreted by experts called *ulema*. They study the Koran and its meaning in order to give legal judgment on any issue. Staunch believers insist that any problem, legal or otherwise, can be solved by consulting the Koran. In Saudi Arabia and some of the Gulf states *sharia* is the only law which applies. Elsewhere there is a secular legal code which has grown up alongside the religious law.

▲ The courtyard of the Ummayyad Mosque, Damascus. Ritual requires that Muslims must wash their hands and feet before praying. All mosques have fountains or containers of water available. The bigger ones are particularly beautiful with their fountains splashing soothingly in the shade of the courtyard. The mosque itself provides a quiet, cool sanctuary from the heat of the day and the noise of the city. It is not surprising that many people spend hours there, not only praying but meditating, dreaming, and even sleeping.

▼ Muslims must pray at five specified times a day, starting at sunrise and finishing late in the evening. They always pray facing the direction of Mecca, kneeling and touching the ground with their foreheads in submission to Allah. They go to the mosque when they can, but this is not necessary. At the appointed hours it is quite common to see workers on a building site, or even farmers in their fields and truck drivers on major highways, unroll a prayer rug or simply kneel down in a quiet spot to perform their sacred rites.

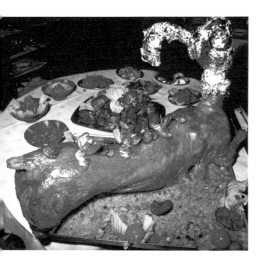

▲ The traditional meal which celebrates the end of Ramadan, the ninth month of the Muslim year. During Ramadan the faithful are required to practise self-sacrifice and special devotions. These take the form of fasting and extra prayer. Muslims do not eat or drink from sunrise to sunset during this period. Because Islam follows a lunar calendar, the month of Ramadan falls at a different time each year. The fast becomes particularly difficult when it is during the hot summer months. In the big cities the hectic pace of life makes it even more exacting. In some countries a canon is fired indicating the moment to eat, at which the whole family participates together in the one meal of the day. This involves special foods and sweets, which are especially rich and nourishing in order to keep people going during the rest of the day. At the end of Ramadan there is a celebratory feast. Each family slaughters and cooks a lamb for the occasion. This is served with other special dishes, particularly sweets.

The people of the Middle East

The Arab majority

To call all the people of the Middle East 'Arabs' would be quite wrong. The first Arabs were people who originally inhabited the Arabian uplands, in what is today Yemen. The term has come to be applied to all the people of the Arabian peninsula, and to those beyond it who speak the Arabic language. As Islam developed and spread through the area, so the Arabic language and culture spread with it.

Minorities and refugees

Many groups, among them Christians and Jews, refused to convert to Islam and continued to practise their religion. Throughout the area there are small communities and ethnic minorities which have retained aspects of their traditional culture.

Until the creation of Israel there were thriving Jewish communities in a number of countries in the Middle East. As hostility between Israel and the Arab states increased, however, these communities were encouraged to emigrate to Israel. In some cases they were intimidated into leaving. There are still some small groups living and working in places like Lebanon, Iraq, Syria and Egypt.

The Assyrians in Iraq and Syria, the Circassians in Syria and the Nubians in Egypt all pre-date Islam. They have managed to retain some aspects of their language and heritage over the centuries.

In Lebanon, Egypt and Syria there are sizeable Armenian communities. Their members fled to these countries in the wake of the terrible Turkish massacre of the Armenians in 1915.

When the state of Israel was established in Palestine, huge numbers of Arabs fled to the neighbouring states. Now unable to return, they live in camps and ghettos in Egypt, Jordan, Syria and Lebanon.

In Israel, as well as the native Palestinian Arabs still living there, there are many Shephardic or oriental Jews who have lived in the area for hundreds of years. The Arab Jews, as they are also known, were previously highly integrated into the Arab culture and they have tended to remain a separate entity within the new state. The new Jewish immigrants have come from all over the world. Some of them were themselves refugees from European fascism in the 1930s, or came after the Second World War, having survived the horrors of Nazi concentration camps in which six million Jews were killed.

Iran and the Gulf

In Iran the largest single group of people are of Persian descent. Though they adopted Islam, they retained their language (which is called Farsi) and many aspects of their ancient civilization. Modern Iran also includes a number of minority groups. These include the Azerbaijanis, who speak a Turkic language, and the Kurds, who speak a language similar to Farsi. There are also the Bakhtiars, the Qasqai and the Turkomans, all of whom are Turkic minorities, as well as Arabs, Armenians, Assyrians and Baluchis, all of whom speak their own languages.

The blossoming industries of the Gulf have attracted immigrants from all over the Middle East and beyond. Some bedouin Arabs from the barren interior have now settled in the growing cities near the coast. Many Egyptians have left their own country, some of them permanently, in order to enjoy the high pay and more spacious living conditions. For some Palestinians the Gulf has provided jobs and an escape route from over-crowded refugee camps. Many of the skilled and semi-skilled labourers in the area are Palestinians.

There is also an ever-growing community of people from the Indian sub-continent. Whole families have settled there and there are now many people of Asian descent who were born in the Gulf.

▶ A Nubian boatman from the Aswan area of Upper Egypt. The Nubians of today are the descendants of a negroid people. They settled in the area and were then conquered by the ancient Egyptians around 3000 B.C., but have retained their own culture over the centuries. When the Nile was dammed at Aswan, the lake which was created (Lake Nasser) flooded much of the Nubian homeland. Villagers were moved to other areas, but for the ancient Nubian culture it was a great loss.

◀ Kurdish women wearing their traditional costume. The Kurds, a people of Indo-European origin, have for centuries occupied the area where Turkey, Iraq, Iran and Syria meet. They are a nation without a country. They have retained their own culture, traditions, and language but they have no autonomy in the states in which they live. Twice in the last 50 years the Kurds have attempted to achieve national recognition. The first time was in 1945, when the Kurdish National Republic was established in Mahabad, Iran. It lasted only one year. The second was in 1974 after a long and bitter struggle in Iraq. The Kurdish Autonomy Law was passed, giving extensive cultural and political rights to those living in the region of Kurdistan in north-eastern Iraq. In practice these concessions meant little. In Lebanon there is a community of about 50,000 Kurds who are free to organize themselves politically and publish their own literature. Government estimates put the Kurdish population at about 11 million, though the Kurds themselves say it is 17 million.

▼ A young woman from Yemen. Yemen's history dates back to well before Islamic times when a thriving civilization prospered and the famous Queen of Sheba ruled. The people of the Yemeni highlands in the south-west of the Arabian peninsula are considered to be the original Arabs, though the name is now used to describe people from other parts of the Middle East. They adopted Islam in the seventh century but have always retained certain aspects of their original culture, including a unique style of dress and building. The rural women wear bright, colourful clothes, and have never worn the veil.

▲ A man from the Gulf coast of Arabia, where many of the old traditions remain and are cherished. The people of the Arabian peninsula migrated towards the coast in search of pasture and water. Some settled and became fishermen or pearl divers and merchants, others continued their nomadic life in the desert areas. The older people, especially, still enjoy the desert pastimes of hunting and falconry. It is not unusual to find falconers, with their noble birds perched on their arms. On some local airlines special facilities are afforded to man and bird.

◀ A Syrian student at Damascus University. Contrary to the popular image of Arabs as dark-skinned and dark-eyed people, there are a great many fair-haired, blue-eyed Arabs, especially in Syria, Lebanon and Palestine. These are descended from the Crusaders who inter-married with the Arabs and stayed on in the area after their defeat in the 12th century.

Food and entertainment

The tradition of hospitality

All Middle Easterners attach the greatest importance to hospitality. A guest must be fed the best that is available. If a bedouin stumbled across a stranger in the desert, it would be a matter of honour to take the stranger home to a feast.

Even today in the cities, it is still the custom to honour guests by inviting them home for a meal. More often than not, enough food is provided to feed the whole table for several meals.

Imaginative recipes

Though the countries of the Middle East are in many ways quite diverse, food is a great uniter. The recipes cover a wide range and many are highly imaginative. They make maximum use of often limited ingredients, blended with herbs and spices.

Many of these recipes originated with the Turks during their long occupation of the area. Among the poor, a variety of unique dishes made from beans, lentils, chick peas and other nourishing protein-containing pulses are eaten. In Lebanon, Jordan, Egypt and Syria, where vegetables are more easily available, the choice is wider. In the Gulf countries, at least before the days of airfreight and refrigerators, meat, bread, rice and dates were staples.

In all the countries of the Middle East, lamb is consumed in vast

quantities. One famous traditional dish is *kharouf mahshi*, a whole baked lamb stuffed with rice and nuts and flavoured with various spices. In the coastal regions stuffed, baked fish is a universal favourite.

Coffee for all occasions

No meal is complete without coffee. It is often Turkish coffee, a strong concentrated mixture served in tiny cups. This is prepared medium, sweet or 'bitter', according to taste.

One cannot go anywhere in the

▲ Just as in Europe meals sometimes begin with a variety of savoury appetizers, so it is in the Middle East where a selection called *mezza* is offered. This can often include as many as 40 small dishes. One common favourite is *hommos*, which is made from crushed chick peas mixed with *tahini*, a thick, creamy paste made from sesame seeds, olive oil and lemon. Or there is *baba ghanouj* made from baked aubergine, also mixed with tahini, oil and lemon. *Kibbe nayyeh* is a kind of raw lamb which has been finely minced and mixed with onions and spices. *Kibbe* are made from finely minced meat mixed with crushed wheat and formed into hollow balls for frying. There are also nuts, olives and salads. Most of the dishes are eaten with a scoop of bread torn from the flat, Arabic loaves.

▶ Drinking alcohol is forbidden by Islam. It is therefore coffee which is a favourite social drink. Coffee houses, or *qahwa*, are found throughout the Middle East. Often they are simple unadorned cafes where men go to talk and smoke a hubble-bubble pipe or *nargeela*. Women do not usually enter coffee houses. They are the nearest equivalent to the Western pub or bar.

◄ The cinema is a popular form of entertainment in most countries of the Middle East. Though this cinema is ultra-modern, films have been shown in the area since the beginning of the twentieth century. Egypt soon became the centre for Middle-East film-making and today it has one of the world's largest film industries. Arabic-language films from Egypt are sold throughout the region, and compete with the equally popular films from the West. Saudi Arabia is the exception to this fashion for film-going: the cinema is forbidden there by law.

▼ At the funeral procession of the singer Um Kulthum in 1970, millions of mourners lined the streets of Cairo. For years this marvellous Egyptian singer dominated the music scene throughout the Middle East. Even now, years after her death, the magic of her voice still captivates people throughout the region.

Middle East without being offered coffee. Arabic coffee was traditionally brewed by the bedouin over their campfires, but nowadays it is offered from shining vacuum flasks in the most modern offices. Middle Easterners drink several coffees a day. It would be considered an insult by a guest not to be offered coffee. To refuse is sometimes also considered an insult.

Unique music

Music plays an important part in daily life. There is not a single taxi or coffee house without its cassette recorder or radio continuously blaring music. Tape recorders and radios are carried around for parties and picnics, even just for walking down the streets. A good heartrending ballad can almost stop the traffic.

Middle Eastern music has a very special sound and beat. To Western ears it often seems melancholy and out of tune. The instruments have changed little over the centuries. They are in fact the forerunners of a number of familiar Western instruments such as the lute, violin, guitar and zither.

One form of entertainment unique to the Middle East is the belly dance. This strange dance is very physically demanding on the women who perform it. A good dancer must have a good sense of rhythm and be in excellent shape. The best receive superstar treatment and can earn a fortune.

33

Science and medicine

Ancient skills

From the earliest times, the people of the Middle East had a knowledge of medicine, astrology, architecture and engineering. Some of their feats baffle scientists to this day. The mystery of the Egyptian pyramids, built in the years 2700 B.C.-1600 B.C., has still not been solved. Thousands of tests and measurements have been carried out on them. Many theories about their purpose and method of construction have been put forward, but nobody has actually come up with any final answers.

A team of experts from Japan recently tried building a mini-pyramid in Cairo. They used a method which they believed to be the same as that used at the time of the Pharaohs, but the experiment turned out a miserable failure.

Archaeological excavations and the information obtained by deciphering scrolls and tablets show that the early Middle Eastern civilizations were very wealthy and highly cultured. They had a wide-ranging vocabulary, a comprehensive legal system and an extensive knowledge of each other's culture.

▲ A 12th century illustration which shows an Arabic chemist making perfume. The Islamic physician Ibn Sina (known to the West as Avicenna) wrote a huge encyclopaedia. It summarized the medical writings of the Greeks, Indians and Persians, and recorded his own experiments and those of his colleagues. Their work covered the fields of surgery, gynaecology, ophthalmology, blood disease and others. He also worked with engineers and astrologers who designed clocks and other scientific measuring instruments. Even by today's standards they remain models of precision and accuracy.

▼ One of many mummified human bodies from the time of the ancient Egyptians which are still preserved today. Scientists and doctors are intrigued by the successful practice of mummification which was invented in the time of the Pharaohs. Some of the mummies have recently been examined to try to discover exactly how this fine and enduring state of preservation was achieved. Even the most modern techniques have failed to reveal the answers. The ancient Egyptians were able to perform certain types of brain surgery, and seem to have had a thorough working knowledge of the body and its functions.

The foundation of modern knowledge

Later, as Islam blossomed, Islamic scholars were able to understand and translate the great works of the Greek, Persian and Indian cultures. To this they added their own findings and extended their research. This knowledge was then translated into Latin and passed on to the West as the Islamic empire spread into Europe. In this way Islamic scholars helped lay the foundations of modern medicine and mathematics, and made important contributions to astrology and engineering.

Hospitals were established in the Islamic empire during the ninth century. Their facilities included outpatient clinics, and in some places there were even mobile field units. There were separate buildings for the mentally sick, who were treated with considerable care and understanding.

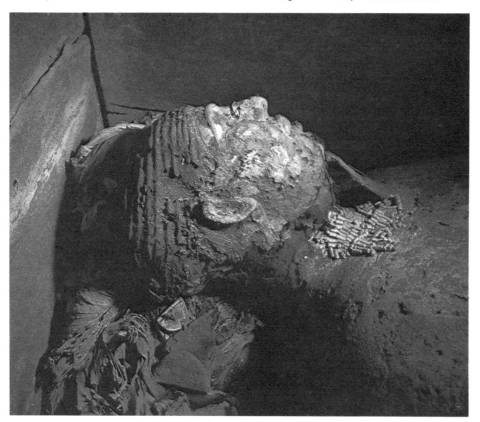

All in all, these hospitals were well in advance of anything seen elsewhere in the world for many centuries afterwards.

Modern technology

The Middle East had lost most of its intellectual ground by the Middle Ages, and has remained well behind the West in science and medicine ever since. Now there is a great determination to catch up. In all technical fields the emphasis is on development and training. Throughout the area, the most sophisticated equipment in the world is being imported, no less in medicine than in engineering or industry.

▶ A primary health-care worker in North Yemen with some of his patients. In many places modern medical care is available only to the wealthy few or not at all. In the poor rural areas many of the people live in unhealthy and insanitary conditions. Serious illnesses, such as gastro-enteritis and tuberculosis, are made worse by malnutrition. The child-killing diseases like poliomyelitis and diphtheria are still common, even though immunization programmes could eradicate them. Most people in these areas have to rely on the traditional cures carried out by village elders. It is in such areas that primary health care is being introduced. Village leaders and volunteer social workers are being taught basic medical skills and personal hygiene which they, in turn, teach their neighbours. The health-care workers learn how to administer immunization against serious disease and can treat minor ailments. They also learn to diagnose severe illnesses at an early stage so that patients can be referred to hospital or a doctor for treatment.

◀ At the newly-opened King Faisal hospital at Riyadh, Saudi Arabia, a nurse keeps watch over her patients by closed-circuit television. Huge amounts of money are being spent on modern medical technology by the oil-producing countries with cash to spend. The King Faisal hospital is one of the most modern in the world, and is run with the help of a vast computer system. It includes a revolutionary cancer treatment centre with its own cyclotron or atom smasher for radiation treatment. Radioactive isotopes are also prepared here for use in the detection and treatment of cancer. Highly sophisticated staff-training programmes use video instruction for teaching surgical techniques.

Education for all

▼ The American University of Beirut, which is universally known as AUB. Together with its medical school and teaching hospital, the AUB has played a major role in the development of the region. It was established in 1886 as a college by Protestant missionaries from the United States. Many of the area's political leaders, skilled professionals and members of the business community have been AUB students. Though the university has suffered badly as a result of the Lebanese civil war, its influence on the region is still considerable.

Religious learning

Though the Middle East boasts the oldest university in the world, the Al-Azhar in Cairo, the development of education has been very sporadic. The Prophet Mohammed taught the people to 'seek knowledge from the cradle to the grave', but it was many years before any recognized schooling system was established.

Education was left in the hands of the parents, and the main emphasis was placed on learning the Koran. For hundreds of years this was the only 'textbook' in use. Eventually a system of private tutors developed. The more enterprising of these gathered several pupils around them in groups which became known as *kuttub* (literally meaning 'books'). These were the first Islamic elementary schools. Apart from the Koran, simple mathematics and a little oral poetry were taught. The pupils were nearly all boys.

The *kuttub* improved gradually but there was still no system of higher education. Again this finally fell under the domain of the private tutor. The founding of the Al-Azhar in 973 marked the beginning of a system of higher education.

Meanwhile, in the rest of the Islamic empire, colleges or *madrassah* were being established. The *madrassah* employed teachers paid by the state. Students received free tuition and sometimes even their board and lodging. With the decline of Baghdad and the Islamic empire generally, this high standard of education also declined.

Western influence

The growth of modern education has been uneven. It started mainly in Egypt under Mohammed Ali in the first half of the nineteenth century. Ali overrode the opposition of the theologians, and opened state secondary schools where mathematics and other subjects were taught by foreign instructors. He also founded colleges of medicine and engineering and sent students to Europe for training.

At the same time, in Syria and Lebanon, Ali's son Ibrahim established a public education system. Catholic and Protestant missionaries were allowed to open schools which eventually developed into important institutions such as the American University of Beirut. Here, in the 1870s, the first girls' schools also began. For a long time the Gulf countries remained cut off from these developments. Educational facilities there were virtually non-existent until the beginning of the twentieth century.

Compulsory education

Today elementary schooling is compulsory in many countries, though the law is not always strictly observed. Since the mid-1950s there has been a new emphasis on building up secondary and higher education. Most important in this area are the technical and vocational training facilities. These are desperately needed to instruct skilled technicians for the jobs which, at the moment, have to be done by specialists from overseas.

▲ The Al-Azhar mosque in Cairo, the oldest university foundation in the world. Al-Azhar is still regarded by Muslim theologians and scholars as the most important authority on Islamic teaching and law. It is still common to see groups of students inside the mosque listening attentively to their teacher instructing them on the Koran. There is also a secular campus in another part of the city. The first national state university was founded in Cairo in 1925. This was soon followed by others as the race to establish national universities began. There are now 40 universities in the Middle East, with new ones opening all the time.

▲ A girls' primary school class in Jidda, Saudi Arabia. Most countries lay down a minimum of six years of schooling for girls, but nine years for boys. In some of the poorer countries, for example Egypt and Syria, parents cannot afford to keep their children in school. Although tuition is free, they do not have the money to pay for uniforms and books. A number of children are forced to leave school so that they can go to work to help maintain their families. The schools themselves have

many problems. In some countries the classrooms are very overcrowded, and basic materials are in short supply. In others, especially the Gulf, money and space is never a problem but there is a shortage of trained teachers. Many of the teachers working there are Egyptians who have temporarily left their own country in search of better pay and conditions. Yet despite all the difficulties, attendance rates are climbing and progress is being achieved.

▶ A class of adults learning to read and write in Damascus, Syria. Compulsory education is relatively new, and is still not always enforced. There are therefore many adults who are illiterate. In most countries there are adult literacy programmes to teach the basic reading and writing skills. Because of the pressures of working and bringing up the family, these classes are often not well attended. Iraq has taken drastic steps to tackle the problem. In 1978 the government decreed that every adult between the ages of 15 and 45 must, by law, attend special literacy classes. Those who do not enrol can be prosecuted. The Iraqis hope that within a few years they will have eradicated illiteracy forever.

Palestine and Israel

▶ A Palestinian refugee camp in Jordan. Many Arabs fled the fighting which broke out in 1948, and took refuge in neighbouring countries. When the fighting stopped, the Israeli authorities prevented them from returning. Over 30 years later many people are still living in camps like this. They are stateless, so they have no passport and no country in which they have rights as nationals. They live mainly by casual work and on the food rations which are distributed to them by the United Nations. Most of the refugees are farmers by tradition. They have resisted attempts to assimilate them into the other Arab countries, in the hope that they will one day be able to return to live on their own land. A million Palestinians still live under Israeli rule in Israel itself and the occupied West Bank.

▲ Ever since the United Nations set out proposals for a Jewish state, Israel has expanded onto its neighbours' territory. In 1956 Israel invaded Egypt in co-operation with Britain and France. Large areas of territory were captured, but were subsequently handed back. The greatest expansion took place during the 1967 war when Israel advanced across Sinai as far as the Suez canal, occupied the Golan Heights in Syria and took over the entire West Bank area, including the Arab section of Jerusalem. In the 'Ramadan' or 'Yom Kippur' war of 1973 Israel was caught off guard. The Arabs made important gains but Israel later recovered most of the lost ground. Since then much of Sinai has been handed back to Egypt, though Israel has kept the Gaza Strip and the city of Gaza. But Arab fears that Israel is bent on expanding its territory at their expense have been strengthened since Israeli Jews have been allowed to settle on Arab-owned land in the occupied areas of the West Bank and the Golan Heights, as well as in Israeli-occupied East Jerusalem.

The Zionist movement

European Jews began to emigrate to Palestine in the 1880s. At that time there were about half a million people living there. Most of them were Arabs, some of whom traced their ancestry back to the Canaanites who occupied the land many centuries before Christ. There was also a Jewish minority of about 30,000 who had lived for centuries in peaceful co-existence with the Arabs.

Jews were being persecuted in many parts of Europe. There was a growing movement, known as Zionism, which was campaigning for a Jewish state to be set up. As support for their cause grew stronger, the Zionists began to insist that a Jewish state should be established in Palestine.

By 1914 the Jewish community in Palestine had doubled to 60,000 while the Arabs numbered 600,000. The Ottomans still ruled Palestine, but at the end of the First World War, in 1918, control passed to Britain. The Balfour declaration of 1917 promised British support for the Zionist cause. The Arabs had not objected to the slow immigration that had been taking place up till then, but they were naturally upset by the idea that a foreign power should wish to set up a state on their own land from which they would be excluded.

Rapid immigration

The pace of Jewish immigration increased over the following 20 years. At first this was supported by the British. A series of riots broke out, and in 1936 there was armed insurrection

by the Palestinians against both the British and the Zionists. Under pressure from the Arabs, the British made some attempts to control the influx of Jews, who were continuing to flee from Europe. Nevertheless conflict continued until the outbreak of the Second World War when all resistance was crushed by Britain.

The birth of Israel

After the war ended in 1945 Britain gave up trying to control the situation. The case was referred to the newly formed United Nations which, in 1947, proposed an end to British rule.

The UN plan called for two states to be set up in Palestine: a Jewish one on 56 per cent of the land, and an Arab one on the remaining 44 per cent. Jerusalem and the holy places were to be placed under UN administration. At this time the Arabs numbered about 1.3 million and the Jews 650,000. The proposal was not accepted by the Arabs.

In May 1948 Israel unilaterally declared itself an independent state. This act provoked the wrath of its Arab neighbours, and war broke out within 24 hours. The fighting lasted until early 1949, by which time Israel held a greatly increased area which included half the city of Jerusalem.

The new state of Israel has become firmly established despite continued opposition on behalf of the Palestinians. In this it has been helped by considerable support from the United States, and by the enthusiasm of many individual supporters from around the world.

Palestinian guerillas in training in Jordan. Despite opposition from most of the countries sheltering them, the guerillas began raids into Israeli territory when hopes of a peaceful settlement faded. Israel replied with reprisals against the countries in which they were based. At the same time the Palestinians launched a campaign of international terrorism, especially hi-jacks. This provoked severe criticism but achieved its aim of publicizing their cause. They also applied political and diplomatic pressure. In 1964 a Palestinian National Council was convened in Jerusalem. The Palestine Liberation Organization was established as a result. The PLO has become the main voice of Palestine, recognized by the United Nations. Palestinians originally demanded that the Jewish state should be disbanded, but some leaders are now pursuing the more limited demand that an autonomous Palestinian state should be set up in Gaza and the West Bank territory.

◀ David Ben-Gurion, Israel's first prime minister. Born in Poland in 1886, Ben-Gurion first went to Palestine at the age of 20. He was expelled by the Turks, but continued to organize support for a Jewish state. He was out of office for a short time in the 1950s, and finally retired as prime minister in 1963.

▼ Prime Minister Begin of Israel (right), President Sadat of Egypt (left) and President Carter of the United States at the signing ceremony of the Camp David agreement, which took place in Washington in 1978. In autumn 1977 President Sadat astonished the world with a proposal that he should visit Israel to discuss the Arab–Israel conflict. Sadat was accused by the rest of the Arab world of betraying the Palestinian cause, but despite an all-out Arab boycott, the Camp David agreement was eventually negòtiated. Among other things this put an end to hostilities between the two countries. Israel agreed to return Egyptian territory captured during previous wars, and they went on to exchange ambassadors.

▲ Packing celery on a communal agricultural settlement or *kibbutz*. For many people the *kibbutzim* represent one of Israel's great successes. The members work together, usually living communally and pooling their resources. Different *kibbutzim* adopt their own style of life and customs. For example, some of them are very strictly religious. These settlements are growing all the time, and their agricultural produce is a valuable export for Israel. But the land they occupy when they grow is often compulsorily purchased from Arab farmers, and the water they take from the rivers may leave little behind for the Arabs' less highly mechanized farms.

Revolution in Iran

Cultural traditions

Apart from Israel, Iran is the only non-Arab state in the Middle East. From the time when Cyrus the Great established the Achaemenid dynasty in 550 B.C., Iran has had a distinct culture with its own language, customs and traditions. These have been maintained even while the country has been occupied by foreign forces. Iran has never been ruled directly by any colonial power, though it came under Russian domination at the turn of this century.

A new dynasty

In 1925 power was taken over by a small military force led by a Cossack officer named Reza Khan. After the takeover he conducted a series of successful campaigns throughout the provinces in which he quashed all opposition. In April 1926 Reza Khan proclaimed himself the first Shah of the Pahlavi dynasty.

Reza Khan saw it as his mission to restore Persia to its former glory and rid it of foreign interference once and for all. To achieve this he built up a strong army which he used to suppress any opposition. He then began a programme of capital construction. Factories, roads and railways were all built in an attempt to develop Iran into a powerful industrial nation.

What this first Shah did not take into account was the growing demands of Iran's neighbour, the Soviet Union. A joint Anglo-Russian force invaded in 1941 and forced Reza Khan into exile. In his place, the throne was given to his 21-year-old son Mohammed Reza.

Plans for modernization

Like his father, the Shah felt he knew what was best for his country and would tolerate no opposition to his plans. He gradually assumed control of all major branches of government.

By 1962 he was pressing ahead with a series of major reforms known collectively as the 'White Revolution'. Many of these, especially the far-reaching land reforms, provoked extensive protests. By 1963 the situation was so bad that the army was called in. Hundreds of people are reported to have been killed.

From this time on, the Shah allowed no opposition. Thousands were arrested, tortured or killed by the secret police, the SAVAK.

Meanwhile he pressed ahead with his modernization plans. Some of the money which flowed in from the sale of oil was used to make the Iranian armed forces among the best-equipped in the world. Iran was one of the first countries to put up the price of oil. With the expected extra wealth, the Shah drew up economic and industrial plans. He believed that Iran would become the world's fifth major power.

While the Shah was putting his ambitious plans into practice, the majority of Iran's 35 million people were gaining very little benefit. Most of them were poor, illiterate, rural workers. Where the changes affected them, it was only to disrupt their lives.

Revolution

As far as many Iranians were concerned, most of the Shah's changes only served to increase the power and wealth of the monarchy and the privileged classes. The gap between rich and poor widened.

Despite the violent and repressive measures of the SAVAK, opposition grew in most sections of the population. Some middle-class people, from whom the Shah had drawn much of his support, turned against him. The clergy played an important part in this opposition. Motivated by a combination of nationalism and religious fundamentalism, they deeply opposed many of the Shah's modern ideas. Often they were encouraged by the strong voice of the exiled Ayatollah Khomeini.

People became increasingly unable to cope with the pressures of the desperately overcrowded cities, housing problems, shortages, inflation and the other side-effects of sudden growth. They turned against the Shah in growing numbers and finally took to the streets. Huge protest marches defied the army and its bullets. They destroyed banks, shops and cinemas, which they saw as decadent symbols of the Shah's regime.

With the powerful army at his command, it was thought at first that the Shah's rule was bound to survive. But the opposition waged unchecked till eventually, on 15 January 1979, the Shah fled his country. Within weeks Ayatollah Khomeini returned in triumph to Iran. Prime Minister Bakhtiar, the last to be appointed by the Shah, also fled soon afterwards and Khomeini became the effective leader of his country.

▲ Shah Mohammed Reza, the second and possibly the last ruler from Iran's Pahlavi dynasty. Though he became ruler in 1941, the Shah staged a lavish coronation ceremony in 1967 to which foreign heads of state, including many other monarchs, were invited. He is seen here, during the ceremony, seated on the famous Peacock throne. Unlike many monarchs, the Shah was not simply a ceremonial leader but the absolute ruler of his country. His plans for modernizing Iran were intended to make it a major industrial power. Popular opposition eventually caused his downfall. Despite being backed by an army equipped with some of the world's most sophisticated weapons, his rule came to a humiliating end in 1979, when massive strikes and street demonstrations throughout the country forced him into exile.

▼ The Kish Island project was one of a number of ambitious tourism and leisure centres, though it was barely complete by the time the Shah fell from power. These super-luxurious hotels, bars and night-clubs were intended to attract affluent jet-setters from all over the world. Some of them belonged to the Shah's immediate family, who also profited from gambling casinos in direct contravention of the laws of Islam. The Revolutionary Council, which governed Iran in the period immediately after the Shah's downfall, closed many of these lavish hotels. The extravagant palaces and museums built by the Pahlavi foundation were placed under lock and key by the Council so that their contents could be inventoried.

▲ Students and religious leaders played an important part in the revolution which shook Iran in 1978–79. Their voices were added to those of the poor, who lived in miserable conditions in the overcrowded cities. Though industries, the transport system and the army benefited from the most modern technology, Tehran still had no proper sewerage system. The feeling of injustice grew when costly international cultural events, such as the annual Tehran film festival, were held to bring prestige to the city. Another group whose opposition led to the Shah's downfall were the *bazaaris*. These prosperous merchants, who handled the lucrative bazaar trade, found their control over the city's trade diminishing.

▼ Ayatollah Khomeini, who at the age of nearly 80 was the leading figure in the Iranian revolution. Khomeini is a devout Muslim who follows absolutely the word of the Koran. His involvement was part of the revival in the political influence of Islam which reached far beyond Iran itself. As leader of the Revolutionary Council he was the most influential leader in Iran from the time the Shah left until a parliament was elected in 1980. He strongly opposed the influence of foreign powers in Iran, and held the United States responsible for supporting the Shah's regime. His supporters seized the US embassy, and imprisoned its staff, in an attempt to force the return of the Shah to stand trial.

Archaeology and architecture

The archaeological legacy

The complex history of the Middle East has left the area with a wealth of archaeological relics. Each of the many civilizations which have flourished in the area left behind the remains of its cities and monuments.

Many governments are now sponsoring extensive conservation and restoration programmes to safeguard these antiquities for the future. National pride is one motive for this work, but there are more tangible benefits too from the tourist industry which grows up alongside.

A distinctive style

Throughout the Middle East a distinctive style of Islamic architecture can be found. The nomadic Arabs had no need for buildings, and therefore no architectural style of their own.

As the Islamic empire spread through the Middle East it was able to draw on the building styles of the Greeks, the Romans and the Byzantine empire, whose buildings they found throughout the area. Within a short time a characteristic style appeared. It draws on old styles, while adapting the design and materials to suit the prevailing climate.

Making the best of the climate

High ceilings, small windows and thick walls provide a cool interior even in the heat of the desert. The best houses are often built on a square, facing inwards towards a shaded central courtyard. Where water is available a fountain splashes soothingly into the bowl beneath. The windows are often set back behind carved shades. These not only provide protection from the sun but also allow the people inside to look out without being seen.

Domes, arches and the intricate painted or carved decorations known as arabesques are all now common features of the Islamic architectural style. They were probably first adopted from the Turks or Byzantines, but soon became an essential feature of the mosques and palaces which took pride of place in any town or city.

▲ The strange, rose-red city of Petra in Jordan. Hidden away by a threatening rock barrier 50 metres high, Petra is a unique archaeological site. It was founded in the 5th century B.C. by the Nabateans who migrated to Jordan from Arabia. As well as being their capital city, Petra became an important caravan stop on the route between the Mediterranean and the Red Sea. The only access to the city was through a long narrow gorge, about three kilometres long and only a few metres wide. From this superb defensive site the Nabateans were easily able to protect themselves. They withstood numerous attacks, and Petra remained a strong, independent seat of the local dynasties even when the Romans occupied the area. The city was then ignored for many centuries, hidden away behind its protective rock barrier. To the Europeans, who stumbled across it in the early 19th century, Petra was an almost unbelievable sight. Palaces, temples, dwellings and other buildings were there, with ornate facades hewn from the deep red rock. Most of them were intact, untouched by the elements or by human destruction. The Jordanian government is now in the process of restoring Petra completely. When it is finished it should be one of the most important sites in the area.

▲ The Petromin University of Dhahran, Saudi Arabia, shows how effectively modern architects have blended old styles and modern materials. The university stands on a hillside to catch the wind, and faces inwards towards cool, green, artificially watered gardens. Its windows are set back, protected by long colonnades with pointed arch supports. The roof is decorated by a series of small, gentle domes. Even the water tower copies the form of a minaret. Arab architects and city planners are turning more to traditional styles, having found that much of the hasty building which took place along Western lines was not a success.

▲ Wind towers, like these in Dubai, are one example of the ways in which Arab architecture makes the best of a hostile climate. Though the weather is hot and dry, the wind towers capture the breeze whenever it blows and direct it through vents into the houses below. In large buildings like this the wind towers form an elegant part of the structure. Smaller buildings often have a more economical, makeshift arrangement of wood and cloth which works just as well. Some old wind towers were adapted as windmills. The force of the wind was used to turn a large fan inside, which in turn drove the machinery below.

▼ These relics of ancient Egypt were the work of several different cultures. They survived for thousands of years on the island of Philae in the middle of the Nile. When the high dam at Aswan was built, the huge artificial lake which formed behind it threatened to submerge the unique monuments. A world-wide appeal was launched for money to save them. Water already covered the island when work began. A temporary barrier was built, and the water was pumped away while a new site was being prepared on an artificial island nearby. The monuments were dismantled stone by stone and then re-erected on their new site.

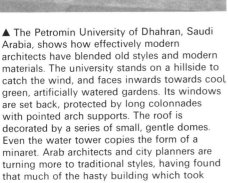

Women's changing roles

Educational opportunities

Since the turn of the century increasing numbers of women in the Middle East have been able to enjoy the benefits of education. This trend began in Egypt and Lebanon, where the first female students were admitted to missionary schools in the late 1800s. Some of these early pioneers forged ahead with such determination that by the beginning of the 1900s several had entered university.

Women have not yet managed to obtain equal treatment with men, but the gap is closing. Even in the conservative Gulf states and Saudi Arabia, educational opportunities are opening up for women.

Equality at work

When it comes to working conditions, women in the Middle East might be surprised at their Western sisters' struggles to gain equality. According to the laws in these countries there should be absolutely no discrimination against women in employment, or in the pay that they receive. Women are automatically allowed maternity leave, and their jobs are kept open for them while they are having a baby. When a mother returns to work she is

▲ Veiled women demonstrating in Iran at the time of the revolution. Whether or not women should always wear a veil in public places is a question which is still hotly disputed. Though the custom that a woman must cover her face in public is today associated with Islam, veiling dates back much further. At the time of the Prophet it was relatively unusual though it became more widespread after the Turkish conquest. The ex-Shah of Iran campaigned *against* the wearing of the veil. For that reason his opponents adopted it as a symbol of freedom, despite its repressive implications in other respects.

▶ In the past there have been no rules and regulations to govern the working conditions of groups such as these women working in the Iranian countryside. It has often been expected that women work with their men without getting paid. Today, as women insist on their legal rights, their position is improving.

allowed an extra hour off during the day to feed her child.

Nevertheless there are still many places, such as Saudi Arabia, where women are expected to choose only certain professions, such as teaching or nursing.

Marriage and divorce

Women's rights within the family are widely misunderstood by outsiders. According to the Koran, a woman has as much right to divorce her husband as he has to divorce her, although she has to make sure that this is provided for in her marriage contract. At the time of her marriage a woman is given a dowry by her husband. This gift becomes her property, and she keeps it even if she is widowed or divorced.

However, the laws are not always applied literally. It takes a determined woman to tackle the male-dominated legal system and get her rights. In practice it is much easier for a man to divorce his wife than the other way round. It is the father, not the mother, who receives custody of the children after a certain age.

Under Islamic law a man is allowed to have up to four wives at once. The law requires him to provide for them all and treat them all equally. It originates from a time when women were entirely dependent on men for their food, shelter and everything else. Polygamy was advocated by the Prophet as a way of making sure that widows and orphans were provided for and protected. Nowadays polygamy is becoming less common.

The veil

The total subservience of women is symbolized for many people by the wearing of the veil. There have always been women who have refused to wear the veil, for example in the rural areas where it got in the way of their work. It became a subject of great controversy in the early part of this century when it came to be regarded as a symbol of oppression. It was violently rejected by the radicals of the time amidst much protest.

Today the veil has almost disappeared from the streets in some of the cities, though it is still worn extensively throughout the Gulf and Saudi Arabia. There are many women who would like to stop wearing it, but prevailing public opinion is still adamant that it should continue to be used.

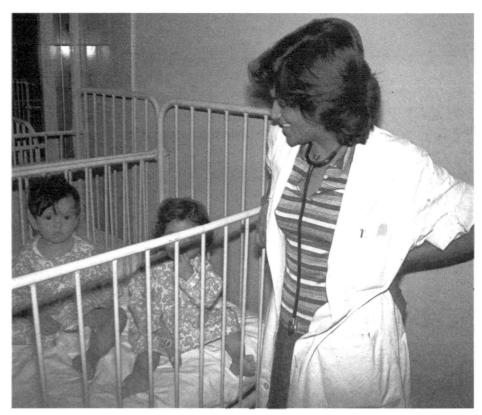

▲ A doctor at work in Kuwait. Even when other professions were denied to women in the Middle East, nursing was accepted. For a long time it was regarded as the only road to higher education. Nowadays, not only nurses but doctors, midwives, and other health specialists are trained in all branches of medicine and are encouraged to follow their profession in hospitals throughout the region. Medicine is one of the most popular professions among women along with teaching, television and journalism.

▼ Policewomen operating in the control room of the Omani police force. In many parts of the Middle East, women fought alongside their menfolk in the struggle for national independence. They were not willing to go back to a subservient role once the immediate struggle was over. In Iraq, Syria, Israel, Jordan, Lebanon and Egypt, women are employed at all levels, including the army and police force. This trend is now reaching even the Gulf. There are some state-run nurseries to take care of the children while their parents are at work.

The flourishing arts

Abstract art

The traditional arts of the Middle East take the form of stunning decorative designs called arabesques, colourful pottery, mosaics and ceramics. They have flourished for many centuries. By contrast it is only in the last hundred years that the performing and modern arts have developed.

The main reason for this was that the Islamic religion forbade any form of representational art. This dates back to Mohammed's doctrine that only Allah can create life. Nobody was therefore allowed to produce a living image.

Subtle poetry

Poetry was among the earliest arts to flourish. Most people could not read and write. The verses were passed on by word of mouth and embellished as they went. Later, when people became literate, the poetry was recorded for posterity.

Both the Arabic and Persian languages are rich in meaning, and great pride is attached to a fine poem. Some words, such as those meaning horse, lion, desert, and especially the words used in praise of Allah, have literally hundreds of different forms. These subtleties of meaning are used for poetic effect.

Calligraphy and arabesques

As writing developed, so did the specialized art-form of calligraphy. It is based on elaborate forms of the beautiful shapes of the Arabic alphabet which are combined into a unified design. This developed along five styles and became increasingly complicated. It started with the copying and reproduction of the Koran. Beautiful illuminated copies were produced. Later, calligraphy was used in the form of friezes and other kinds of decoration on mosques and holy places.

Arabesques are based on complicated geometric patterns. They are put together as mosaics or ceramic tiles in bright colours. Arabesques embellish both public and private buildings. The arabesques can be seen as the first stages of abstract art. They had a profound effect on the Western painters who first saw them and inspired early Western schools of modern art.

Similar shapes and patterns are also found in the beautiful Arabic and Persian rugs. They brighten up homes, mosques and public buildings throughout the Middle East, and are in strong contrast to the stark, desert landscapes all around.

◄ A design in the shape of a pear by the modern Iraqi calligrapher Hashem al-Khattat. The right-hand leaf is made up from the words 'I take refuge in God against the accursed devil.' It is written in the script called *Thuluth*, which was formulated in the seventh century. The body of the pear consists of a passage from the Koran in *Thuluth*. The lines below it are a continuation of the same passage, but in a different style of script called *Nashki*. It is part of the calligrapher's skill that every single line is part of the script, even including those lines which appear at first sight to be outlines.

► A craftsman displays his jewellery. The bedouin Arabs kept very few possessions, but jewellery was one way in which wealth could be conveniently invested. It took many forms, including necklaces, bracelets, anklets, pendants, earrings, rings and heavy embossed belts. The work was decorated with semi-precious stones or delicate filigree work, bells and other trinkets. Amulets were worn to bring good luck. Those in the form of an eye or a hand were especially popular. It used to be the custom for jewellery to form part of the dowry which a woman received from her husband. Styles of jewellery have changed over the years, but the tradition of buying and wearing jewellery is still as strong as ever.

◄ The London opening of an exhibition of paintings by Iraqi artists. As painters from the West began to visit the Middle East they were struck by the unfamiliar sights and landscapes. They began to incorporate them into their work, which in turn influenced would-be artists in the Middle East. The first movements began in Egypt and Iraq, whose governments have since done a great deal to encourage painting. A number of young artists have been sent abroad to study. Although strongly influenced by European styles at first, these artists have used their own themes to develop a distinctive Middle Eastern school. As the struggle for independence grew, and support for the Palestinian movement increased, some artists took up a strong military theme which still continues.

◄ A play on stage in Qatar. Theatre developed in the Middle East alongside Arab nationalism, whose leaders saw it as an effective way of getting their point across in a mixture of entertainment and political instruction. The theatre movement began in Egypt in the 1920s and reached its height in the 1950s and 1960s under Nasser. It became strong in Iraq and Syria during the fight for independence in the years after the Second World War. Theatre is such a powerful means of expression that today it is suffering from the heavy hand of censorship in many of the countries where it once flourished. Despite conservative opposition to the idea of theatre, it is now being officially encouraged in many of the Gulf states. Elaborate theatres are being built, and local playwrights and actors are given every encouragement.

Sports old and new

Competitive sport

Until the mid-1920s, competitive sport as it is known in the West was almost unheard of in the Middle East. Races, both for camels and horses, have been held in the desert for centuries and there was fierce rivalry among the bedouin over their horses. Hunting and falconry were also taken seriously. Owners of the best birds acquired considerable prestige.

Organized sporting activities were introduced by Christian missionaries. Track and field athletics, tennis and swimming were part of the curriculum of their colleges in Lebanon and Syria. People slowly began to take an interest, but the big boost came with the influx of European troops during the First World War. The soldiers enjoyed a friendly game of soccer, and when they left the local people took up the game themselves.

A passion for soccer

Soccer was first adopted by the Egyptians, for whom it is now a national passion. The Nasser stadium in Cairo holds crowds of over 120,000. Egyptian soccer teams took part in the World Cup as early as the 1920s.

In terms of popularity throughout the region, football is number one, followed by basketball, volleyball, weight-lifting, swimming, tennis and squash. Tennis has been established in the area for many years. Egypt, Lebanon and Syria have all sent contestants to Wimbledon.

Squash is new, but has quickly become popular. In the Gulf states air-conditioned courts make it one of the few all-year-round sports. Gymnastics is gaining momentum for the same reason. In the coastal regions, many people are taking up sailing. In Lebanon water skiing is already a popular pastime.

Competition and recreation

Although there are millions of swimmers, competitive swimming is a fairly new concept. The Egyptians have been competing internationally for several years. They have a good record in the long-distance events. Some of their swimmers have broken international records. In 1974, teen-ager Abla Khairi became the youngest swimmer to cross the English Channel.

Golf is another popular innovation. There have been courses in Egypt and Lebanon since the 1940s. More recently it has caught on in other countries, including Saudi Arabia. Here the courses are rough and sandy. The balls are bright red to make them easy to spot in the glaring sun.

For such a hot, dry climate perhaps the strangest sport of all is ice-skating, the latest craze to hit the Gulf. In the last few years several rinks have opened. In the mountains of Syria and Lebanon skiing is slowly becoming popular.

Many governments invest heavily in sporting facilities and are doing a lot to encourage young people to participate.

▲ Wrestling is a popular sport throughout the Middle East, as these posters in Beirut show. It is one of the world's oldest sports too, and engravings have been found in Egypt depicting wrestlers of Pharaonic times. Iran is perhaps the foremost country for wrestling, and it is a major spectator sport there. Iranian wrestlers have been successful in many international competitions and have won a number of Olympic medals. Weight-lifting is a related sport which also relies on physical strength. The Lebanese champion Mohammed Trabulsi is a world-class performer.

▲ A camel race in Saudi Arabia. Informal camel racing has been part of desert life for centuries. These days the sport is a bit more organized, and usually takes place on the tracks outside the main cities in the late afternoon. Betting is absolutely forbidden by Islamic law, but that does not reduce the excitement of the event. Horse racing has recently been introduced in the Gulf. The annual King's Cup race in Saudi Arabia has the same pomp and formality as equivalent events in other parts of the world.

▼ In 1979 the Saudi Arabian national airline, Saudia, began to sponsor Grand Prix racing cars on the international circuits. The car was driven by foreign professionals, but it may not be long before Arab drivers take over. Motor racing is the sport of the future for the Middle East. Rich youngsters in the Gulf states spend their leisure time and substantial pocket money on fast cars, which they drive at speed on the open desert roads. International car rallies held in the area have drawn an enthusiastic response both at home and overseas. The young Kuwaiti rally driver Tariq Wazzan has already made a name in international events.

▲ A soccer match under way in Riyadh, the Saudi capital. Soccer is by far the most popular spectator sport throughout the Middle East. The richer countries are putting a lot of money and effort into improving their teams. New stadiums are being built, many of them equipped with powerful floodlights so that the games can be held in the cool of the evening. A number of famous foreign players have accepted positions as trainers and managers, helping to develop the national teams. Their experienced instruction is paying off. There are thousands of amateur players too. Every state, no matter how small, now has its own league.

▼ Backgammon may not be as energetic as other games but the competitive spirit can be just as fierce. The game has been played in the Middle East for at least 5,000 years, and is known there as *tric-trac* or *tawle*. It is probably one of the most widespread leisure pastimes in the area, and is played by men everywhere in the coffee houses and out on the pavement. It is a basic day-to-day game, played with simple boards and equipment. This contrasts with the lavish kits and complicated instructions which appeared in the West when the game became popular there a few years ago.

Looking to the future

Coming of age

Most Middle Eastern countries did not achieve legal independence until the end of the Second World War. Even then both French and British influence remained strong in the area. Effective independence did not come about until well into the 1950s, and in some cases even later. Even today, foreign influence is still obvious in some countries.

The Middle East came of age rather suddenly during the 1970s, starting with the 1973 war between Israel and her Arab neighbours.

With this war came a double realization. Israeli troops were beaten back from the Suez canal by the Egyptians, and with this the myth of Israeli invincibility was shattered. Even more important, the Arab states realized that the oil they supplied to the rest of the world could be used to exert political influence. Not only could they demand a fair price for their oil; they could also threaten to withhold supplies for political reasons. For a short time in 1973 they stopped supplying oil to certain states whom they believed to be helping Israel.

The Arabs finally began to shake off their inferiority complex born of centuries of foreign domination, and to develop their potential both as individual countries and as a regional power.

Continuing problems

Nevertheless, the Middle East is beset with problems. There are extremes of wealth and poverty, and a multitude of cultural minorities are striving for recognition.

The governments themselves represent the full range of political ideologies. They range from extreme left to extreme right: from Soviet-backed communism, through Arab socialism to absolute monarchy. Many countries have passed from a totally sheltered, traditional lifestyle into a position of enormous wealth within a generation, and the people have not yet had time to adjust.

The Islamic movement

The effect of the Islamic revival, which began in Iran with the overthrow of the Shah, is being felt throughout the area and beyond. In some places it is taking the form of a conflict between the Sunni and Shia Muslim sects. Elsewhere Muslim purists attack, sometimes with actual force, anything they consider to be too liberal or Westernized.

The old idea that the West is best is being seriously questioned. Many of the younger people have already recognized the potential strength and wisdom to be gained from their own culture. They are now challenging their parents' pro-foreign attitudes.

A very serious threat to peace still lies in the conflict between Israel and Palestine. Despite their differences, all the countries of the Middle East recognize that there can never be peace in the area until this question is resolved.

◄ International groupings of many kinds, such as this conference of Islamic nations, are strengthening the position of the nations of the Middle East. Despite the political differences which separate the countries of the region, there is still a strong feeling of common purpose over certain issues. From time to time the heads of government of all the Arab states, including those in North Africa, meet to discuss matters of common interest. The Baghdad summit in 1978 attempted to define the powers and aims of the Arab Middle East.

► This television studio in Qatar shows one of the many ways in which the Middle Eastern states are adapting modern high technology to meet their own needs. Progress in education, the social services, transport and communication is improving the lives of many people throughout the region. Foreign products and skills are adapted to suit local conditions. For example, the successful American children's programme *Sesame Street* has been completely re-made for an Arab audience. Before being transmitted it was tested and re-tested. It has a potential audience of over 25 million children of pre-school age all over the Arab Middle East.

◀ Sheikh Yamani is oil minister for Saudi Arabia, one of the most influential members of the Organization of Petroleum Exporting Countries (OPEC). He has played a very important part in explaining the Arab position to the rest of the world. In 1973, after almost 25 years of trying to find a solution to the problem of Palestine, the Arab countries finally discovered a weapon which could help them fight for their cause. It was oil. They threatened to cut off oil supplies to Western countries which unconditionally supported Israel. They cut back production of oil and increased its price to a level comparable with other commodities on the world market. In this way the Arab states were finally able to convince the West that the days of exploitation were over.

▶ Damage in Beirut caused by fighting in the Lebanese civil war, which started in 1975. The conflict arose from internal tensions, but caught up the Palestinian refugees living in the country. The bitter war has lasted into the 1980s, with Christian fighting Muslim and leftist fighting rightist. Other Arab states have become involved, and both the United States and the Soviet Union have indirectly tried to influence events in Lebanon. Israel became involved too, at first by training the Christian rightists. Later, Israel advanced a short way into Lebanon and gave open support to the Christians. Sporadic fighting continued even after an Arab peacekeeping force, consisting mainly of Syrian troops, arrived in the country. Beirut itself has been divided by the war, with different parts of the city occupied by the different factions.

Reference: *Human geography*

▶ Population density varies considerably from place to place in the Middle East. The fertile strip along the Nile valley is one of the most densely populated areas on earth, while the rest of Egypt is very sparsely populated. The desert interior of the Arabian peninsula is also very sparsely populated, and the barren south is practically unpopulated. Only the more fertile upland areas and some of the coasts have a significant number of inhabitants. To the north there are scattered communities throughout northern Syria, Iraq and western Iran, giving a relatively high population density overall.

Inhabitants per km^2

- 100
- 50
- 10
- 1
- unpopulated

Countries of the Middle East

Bahrain
Independent sheikhdom since 1971; previously a British protectorate.
Capital: Manama
Head of state: Sheikh Isa al-Khalifa

Egypt
Republic since 1952; previously an independent kingdom.
Capital: Cairo
Head of state: President Anwar Sadat

Iran
Islamic republic since overthrow of the Shah in 1979; previously an absolute monarchy.
Capital: Tehran
Head of state: President Mohammad Ali Rajai

Iraq
Independent republic since 1958; previously a monarchy since 1932; previously a British mandated territory since 1920.
Capital: Baghdad
Head of state: President Saddam Hussein

Israel
Independent republic since 1948.
Capital: Jerusalem
Head of state: President Yitzhak Navon

Jordan
Independent kingdom since 1946; previously British mandated territory of Transjordan.
Capital: Amman
Head of state: King Hussein

Kuwait
Independent sheikhdom since 1961; previously British protectorate since 1869.
Capital: Kuwait City
Head of state: Sheikh Jabir al-Sabah

Lebanon
Independent republic since 1941; formerly French mandated territory.
Capital: Beirut
Head of state: President Elias Sarkis

Oman
Independent sultanate since 1970; previously linked to Britain.
Capital: Muscat
Head of state: Sultan Qaboos bin Said

Qatar
Independent sheikhdom since 1971.
Capital: Doha
Head of state: Sheikh Khalifa al-Thani

Saudi Arabia
Independent kingdom since 1926.
Capital: Riyadh
Head of state: King Khaled

Syria
Arab republic since 1945; previously French mandated territory.
Capital: Damascus
Head of state: President Hafez Assad

United Arab Emirates
Federation of seven independent emirates: Abu Dhabi, Ajman, Dubai, Fujaira, Ras al Khaimah, Sharja and Umm al Quwain
Capital: Abu Dhabi
Head of state: Sheikh Zaid al-Nahyan

North Yemen
Arab republic since 1962; previously monarchy since 1918.
Capital: San'a
Head of state: President Abdallah Saleh

South Yemen
Popular democratic republic since 1967; previously British colony.
Capital: Aden
Head of state: Chairman Nasser Mohammed

The boundaries of Iran and Egypt correspond roughly to the areas occupied by ancient civilizations. Elsewhere, national boundaries have been determined largely by outside influence. In the north, the boundaries were drawn by the European powers at the end of the First World War. Lebanon and Syria were ruled by France, while Jordan, Iraq and Palestine came under British control. After the Second World War the United Nations further divided Palestine into an Arab and a Jewish state. The new state of Israel later extended its influence throughout Palestine and beyond.

In the Arabian peninsula it was mainly the coastal areas which attracted the European powers' interest. Britain wanted to protect its sea routes to the Far East, and occupied strategic points on the Gulf coast and in the south. British influence continues, especially in Oman. Saudi Arabia is a powerful force, and the coastal states are now all independent. Even so, not all the land boundaries are settled yet, especially in the desert areas.

▶ The areas and populations of the countries of the Middle East.

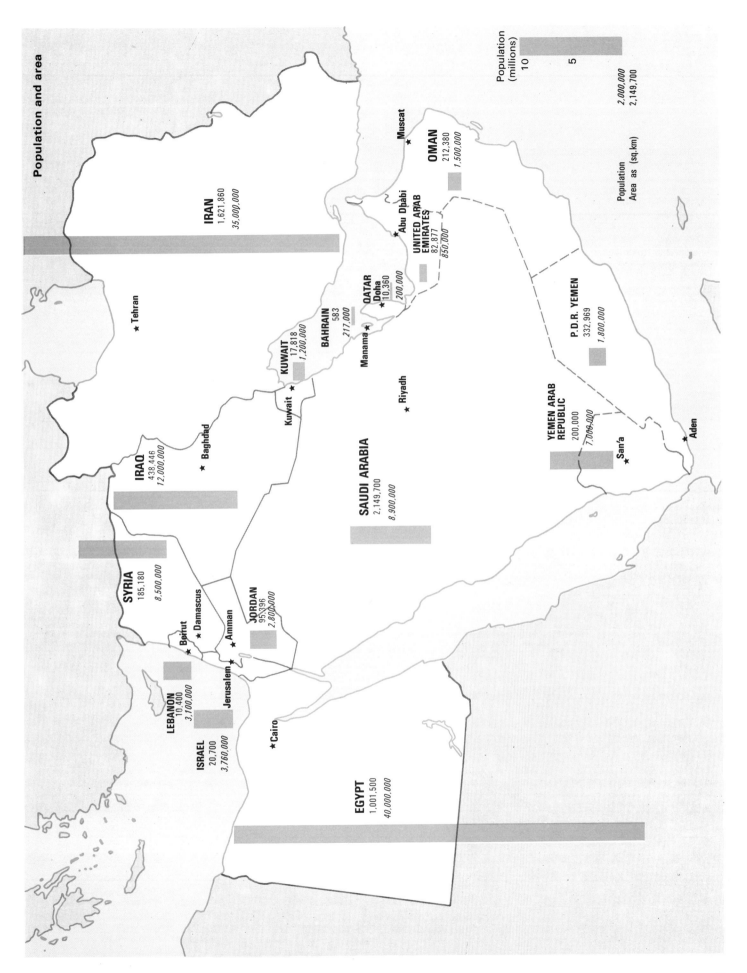

Population and area

Population
(millions)
10
5

Population
Area as (sq.km)
2,000,000
2,149,700

OMAN
212,380
1,500,000

Muscat ★

UNITED ARAB
EMIRATES
82,877
850,000

Abu Dhabi ★

P.D.R. YEMEN
332,969
1,800,000

QATAR
Doha
10,360
200,000

★

BAHRAIN
583
217,000

Manama ★

KUWAIT
17,818
1,200,000

Kuwait ★

Riyadh ★

IRAN
1,621,860
35,000,000

Tehran ★

YEMEN ARAB
REPUBLIC
200,000
7,000,000

San'a ★

Aden ★

IRAQ
438,446
12,000,000

Baghdad ★

SAUDI ARABIA
2,149,700
8,900,000

SYRIA
185,180
8,500,000

Damascus ★

Beirut ★

JORDAN
95,396
2,800,000

Amman ★

LEBANON
10,400
3,100,000

Jerusalem ★

ISRAEL
20,700
3,760,000

Cairo ★

EGYPT
1,001,500
40,000,000

53

Reference: *Climate and agriculture*

▶ Large areas of the Middle East receive less than 12.5 mm (0.5 in) of rain in a year. The eastern Mediterranean coast and the mountains of Iran receive appreciable quantities of rain, most of which falls during the winter months. The pattern is different in the Yemen highlands. Here, most of the rain originates from the monsoons which sweep across the Indian Ocean during the summer months. Temperatures show seasonal variation throughout the area. This is most pronounced towards the north-east where the continental influence of Asia can be felt most strongly.

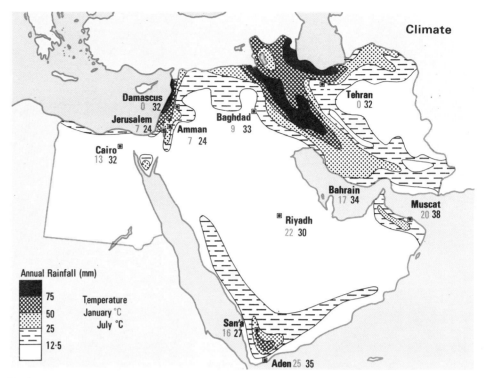

Annual Rainfall (mm)

■ 75	Temperature
▦ 50	January °C
▨ 25	July °C
▤ 12·5	

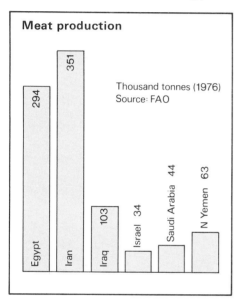

Meat production

Thousand tonnes (1976)
Source: FAO

Egypt 294 · Iran 351 · Iraq 103 · Israel 34 · Saudi Arabia 44 · N Yemen 63

▲ The six main meat-producing countries of the Middle East. Even land which is too dry for crops to be grown can be used to feed grazing cattle.

▼ Employment patterns vary considerably from country to country. In the arid Gulf states agriculture occupies only a small proportion of the workforce, while the fertile areas of Egypt, Iran and Iraq support a large rural population.

Irrigating the desert

Agriculture plays a large part in the life of the Middle East, even though only a small proportion of the land can be cultivated. In Egypt, for example, only 3 per cent of the land can be used, though agriculture is still the country's most important industry.

Irrigation is essential throughout much of the region, and the major rivers provide most of the water used for this purpose. Ground water supplies the wells which irrigate the desert oases.

Food and raw materials

Crops are grown both for food and as raw materials for industry. Grain crops include wheat, barley and rice. Fruit range from apples, cherries and strawberries on the Mediterranean coast, to the date palms which flourish in the desert.

Cotton is a major crop and the basis of the important textile industries.

Fisheries

Egypt 106·6	Total catch (1976) (thousand tonnes) Source: FAO
Iraq 21·8	
Israel 25·8	
Oman 198	
Saudi Arabia 23·3	
UAE 68	
S Yemen 127	

▲ The warm waters of the Mediterranean, the Red Sea and the Gulf provide fertile fishing grounds. These resources are still not fully exploited. The traditional fishing grounds in the Gulf are now being threatened by pollution from industrial development along the coast.

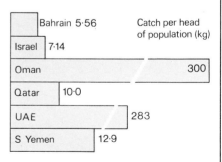

Bahrain 5·56	Catch per head of population (kg)
Israel 7·14	
Oman 300	
Qatar 10·0	
UAE 283	
S Yemen 12·9	

▲ Although a large proportion of the total catch is landed by the larger states, it is in the small countries of the Gulf that fishing makes the most significant contribution to the local economy. Oman continues to export fish, though it has recently been overtaken in importance by oil.

Employment in agriculture

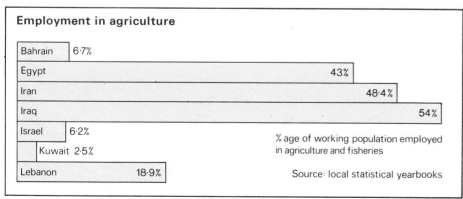

Country	%
Bahrain	6·7%
Egypt	43%
Iran	48·4%
Iraq	54%
Israel	6·2%
Kuwait	2·5%
Lebanon	18·9%

% age of working population employed in agriculture and fisheries

Source: local statistical yearbooks

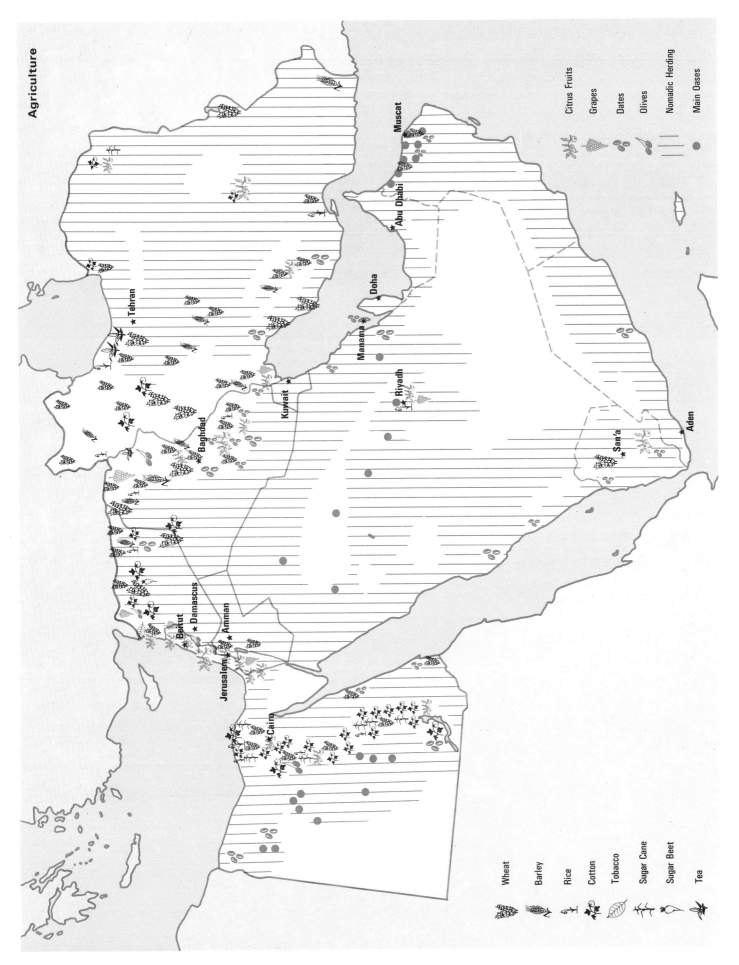

Agriculture

Citrus Fruits
Grapes
Dates
Olives
Nomadic Herding
Main Oases

Wheat
Barley
Rice
Cotton
Tobacco
Sugar Cane
Sugar Beet
Tea

Muscat
Abu Dhabi
Doha
Manama
Riyadh
San'a
Aden
Tehran
Baghdad
Kuwait
Damascus
Beirut
Amman
Jerusalem
Cairo

55

Reference: *Minerals and industry*

Mineral resources

With the conspicuous exception of oil, the Middle East has few mineral resources. The Dead Sea area is a source of salt and potash, which is exported for use in fertilizers. Iran also produces some chrome ore which is exported on the world market. Jordan exports phosphates for use elsewhere in the region; though not important on an international scale, phosphates are Jordan's most valuable single export commodity.

Industries are of two kinds: the traditional industries, and new technologies bought in with the money

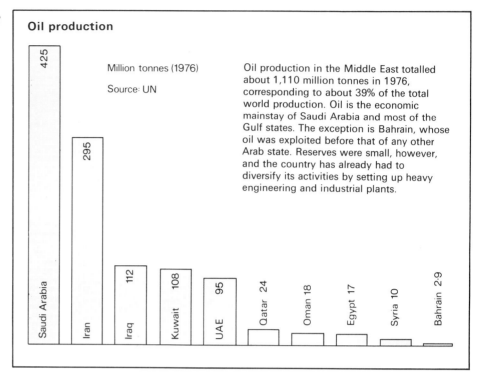

Oil production

Million tonnes (1976)

Source: UN

Saudi Arabia 425
Iran 295
Iraq 112
Kuwait 108
UAE 95
Qatar 24
Oman 18
Egypt 17
Syria 10
Bahrain 2·9

Oil production in the Middle East totalled about 1,110 million tonnes in 1976, corresponding to about 39% of the total world production. Oil is the economic mainstay of Saudi Arabia and most of the Gulf states. The exception is Bahrain, whose oil was exploited before that of any other Arab state. Reserves were small, however, and the country has already had to diversify its activities by setting up heavy engineering and industrial plants.

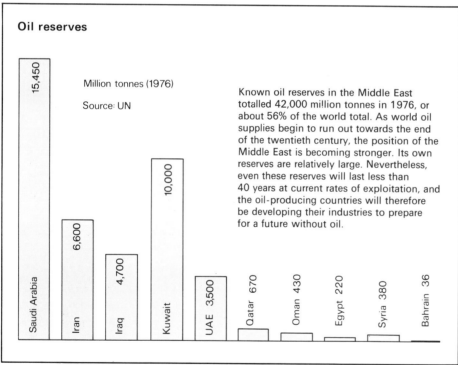

Oil reserves

Million tonnes (1976)

Source: UN

Saudi Arabia 15,450
Iran 6,600
Iraq 4,700
Kuwait 10,000
UAE 3,500
Qatar 670
Oman 430
Egypt 220
Syria 380
Bahrain 36

Known oil reserves in the Middle East totalled 42,000 million tonnes in 1976, or about 56% of the world total. As world oil supplies begin to run out towards the end of the twentieth century, the position of the Middle East is becoming stronger. Its own reserves are relatively large. Nevertheless, even these reserves will last less than 40 years at current rates of exploitation, and the oil-producing countries will therefore be developing their industries to prepare for a future without oil.

obtained from oil exports. The most important of the traditional industries is the manufacture of textiles. Many up-to-date cotton mills have been built in recent years. In Iran, local wool provides the basis for carpet manufacturing.

New industries

Assembly plants are now being constructed where consumer goods are built up from imported components. Heavy industry is also growing. There are a number of steel and cement works throughout the region. Bahrain has recently completed an aluminium smelter.

Though there is hardly any coal in the area, energy is now in abundant and cheap supply from oil. This may be used either directly, or indirectly as electricity. Egypt obtains electrical power from the hydro-electric installation at the Aswan High Dam.

Employment in industry

% age of working population employed in manufacturing industry

Source: local statistical yearbooks

Country	Percentage
Bahrain	14%
Egypt	12·5%
Iran	18·8%
Iraq	6·6%
Israel	24%
Kuwait	9·8%
Lebanon	17·7%

▶ Industry is a relatively minor employer in all the countries of the Middle East. The picture is changing rapidly, however, especially in the oil-producing states.

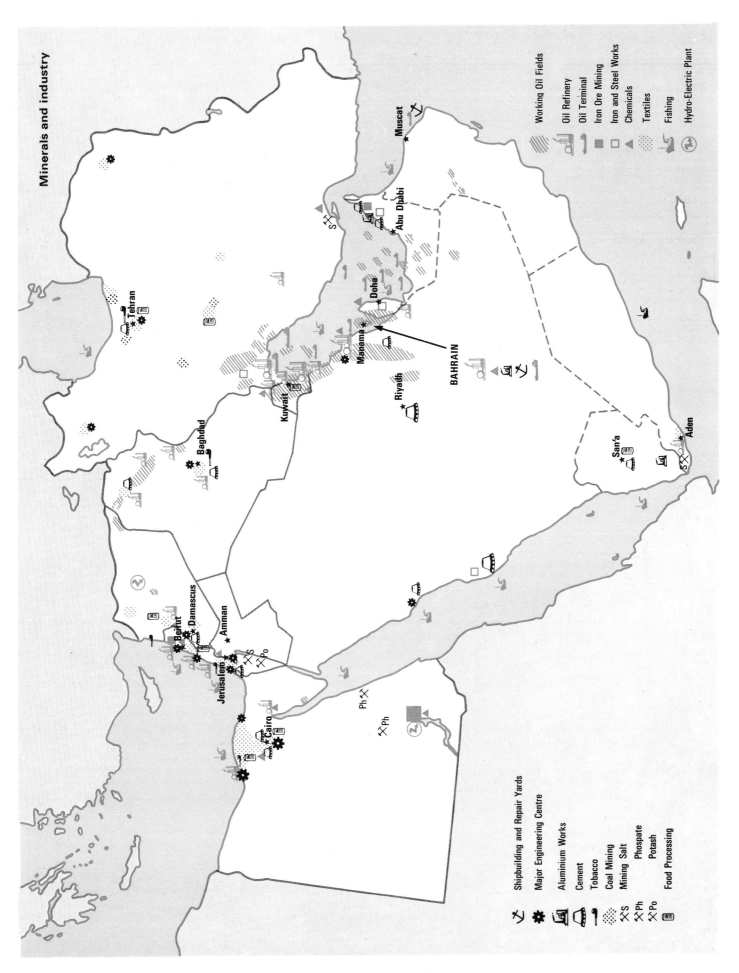

Minerals and industry

Tehran
Baghdad
Kuwait
Riyadh
Doha
Manama
BAHRAIN
Abu Dhabi
Muscat
San'a
Aden
Beirut
Damascus
Amman
Jerusalem
Cairo

Working Oil Fields
Oil Refinery
Oil Terminal
Iron Ore Mining
Iron and Steel Works
Chemicals
Textiles
Fishing
Hydro-Electric Plant

Shipbuilding and Repair Yards
Major Engineering Centre
Aluminium Works
Cement
Tobacco
Coal Mining
Mining Salt
Phospate
Potash
Food Processing

57

Reference: *Wealth and trade*

▶ The international trade of the 15 countries of the Middle East. The value of the trade is given as the total of exports and imports. The main imports and exports are given, and the percentages show the proportion of total imports or exports represented by each commodity. Similarly, the main foreign customers and suppliers are given, together with the proportion of total exports and imports that trade with the foreign country represents. Data are derived from local statistical yearbooks and national bank reports. All figures are for 1977, except Kuwait, Saudi Arabia and South Yemen (1976), North Yemen (1975) and Lebanon (1973).

National currencies

Bahrain
Bahrain dinar: 1 BD = $2.63

Egypt
Egyptian pound: E£1 = $1.44

Iran
Iranian rial: 1 rial = $.0145

Iraq
Iraqi dinar: 1 dinar = $3.40

Israel
sheckel: 1 sheckel = $.16

Jordan
Jordanian dinar: 1 dinar = $3.40

Kuwait
Kuwaiti dinar: 1 dinar = $3.75

Lebanon
pound: L£1 = $.29

Oman
Omani rial: 1 RO = $2.90

Qatar
Qatar rial: 1 QR = $.28

Saudi Arabia
Saudi rial: 1 SR = $.30

Syria
Syrian pound: S£1 = $.26

United Arab Emirates
UAE dirham: 1 dirham = $.28

North Yemen
Yemeni rial: 1 rial = $.22

South Yemen
Yemeni dinar: 1 dinar = $2.95

All exchange rates are commercial rates as of November 1980.

Wealth produced

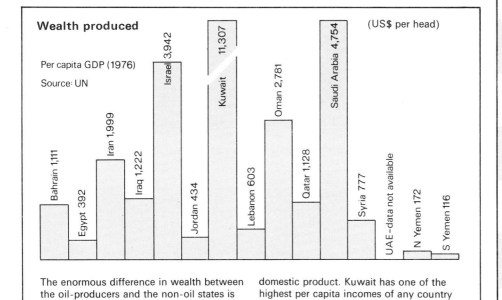

Per capita GDP (1976)
Source: UN

(US$ per head)

Bahrain 1,111 · Egypt 392 · Iran 1,999 · Iraq 1,222 · Israel 3,942 · Jordan 434 · Kuwait 11,307 · Lebanon 603 · Oman 2,781 · Qatar 1,128 · Saudi Arabia 4,754 · Syria 777 · UAE–data not available · N Yemen 172 · S Yemen 116

The enormous difference in wealth between the oil-producers and the non-oil states is shown by the range of per capita gross domestic product. Kuwait has one of the highest per capita incomes of any country in the world.

International trade

Country	Value of international trade (approx. '000,000,000 US $)
Bahrain	4.2
Egypt	2.1
Iran	35.7
Iraq	13.5
Israel	7.7
Jordan	1.7
Kuwait (1976)	15.2
Lebanon (1973)	2.3
Oman	2.4
Qatar	3.3
Saudi Arabia (1976)	61.2
Syria	3.9
United Arab Emirates	not known
North Yemen (1975-76)	0.38
South Yemen (1976)	0.51

Imports	Foreign suppliers	Exports	Foreign customers
Crude petroleum 45% Machinery, etc. 20%	United Kingdom 20%* Japan 16%* United States 12%*	Petroleum products 79% Non-ferrous metals 6% Machinery 4%	Saudi Arabia 52%* Japan 27%* Iran 9%
Food 21% Machinery, etc. 21% Oil 13%	United States 16% W Germany 11% France 6%	Textiles and fibres 47% Crude petroleum 18% Agricultural products 15%	Soviet Union 23% Italy 11% Czechoslovakia 7%
Machinery, etc. 43% Manufactured goods 31% Food and drink 11%	W Germany 19% Japan 16% United States 16%	Petroleum and products 76% Carpets 5% Cotton 4%	Soviet Union 17%* W Germany 15%* United States 8%*
Engineering equipment 14% Cars and parts 12% Sugar 2%	Japan 15% W Germany 13% United Kingdom 6%	Crude petroleum 86% Dates 0.5%	India 16%* China 12%* Vietnam 10%*
Oil 19%** Machinery, etc 17%** Iron and steel 6%**	United States 20% United Kingdom 10% W Germany 9%	Agricultural products 18% Iron and steel 14% Textiles 13%	United States 20% W Germany 9% United Kingdom 8%
Machinery, etc. 34% Minerals 16%	United States 15% W Germany 14% Saudi Arabia 8%	Phosphates 28% Fruit and vegetables 28%	Saudi Arabia 25% Syria 13% Iraq 7%
Machinery, etc. 42% Manufactured goods 20% Textiles 10%	European Economic Community 33% Japan 21% United States 15%	Petroleum and gas 93%	Asia 44% European Economic Community 29% United States 7%
Machinery, etc. 30%** Vegetable products 11%**	W Germany 11% United States 11% France 11%	Textiles 14% Vegetable products 12%	Saudi Arabia 16% France 10% United Kingdom 9%
Machinery, etc. 41% Manufactured goods 27% Food and animals 13%	United Kingdom 23% United Arab Emirates 15% W Germany 6%	Petroleum 99% Fruit and fish 1%	not available
not available	Japan 27% United Kingdom 19% United States 10%	Oil 99% Fertilizer 1%	United Arab Emirates 26%* Saudi Arabia 21%*
Machinery, etc. 45% Foodstuffs 11% Textiles 7%	United States 19% Japan 12% W Germany 8%	Crude petroleum 93% Refined petroleum 7%	Japan 20% France 12% Italy 6%
Minerals and fuel 17% Machinery, etc. 15% Manufactured goods 13%	W Germany 14% Saudi Arabia 11% Romania 9%	Petroleum 58% Cotton 15% Textiles 6%	Italy 13% Soviet Union 10% France 7%
Machinery, etc. 39% Manufactured goods 36% Food 8%	Japan 20% United Kingdom 17% United States 11%	not known	not known
Food 43% Manufactured goods 26% Machinery, etc. 17%	Japan 14% India 9% China 8%	Cotton 48% Hides 16% Coffee 15%	China 4% Italy 17% S Yemen 17%
Petroleum and products 41% Machinery, etc. 10% Cereals 8%	United Kingdom 8%* Japan 6%* Kuwait 3%*	Petroleum products 99% Coffee, tea, etc. 1%	not available

*not including oil
**not including diamonds and precious metals

59

A brief history of the Middle East

Index

B.C.
7000 First settlements in the area of Mesopotamia.

5000–2000 The Sumerian culture flourishes around Mesopotamia.

3000–656 Pharaonic period in Egypt.

1466–1200 Hittites rule in Mesopotamia.

1200–631 Assyrians rule.

631–539 Neo-Babylonians rule.

558–330 The Achaemenid dynasty rules Persia.

356–323 Lifetime of Alexander the Great.

A.D.
221–337 Roman influence strong throughout Middle East.

337–641 Byzantine influence grows strong, especially in Egypt.

571 Mohammed born in Mecca.

622 Mohammed moves from Mecca to Medina; the beginning of the *Hijra* calendar.

632 Mohammed dies.

640 Egypt surrenders to the Muslims.

660–750 Ummayyads lead Islam with their capital in Damascus.

711 Spain and the Indus valley are invaded by the Muslims.

750 Ummayyads are overthrown by the Abbasids.

762 Abbasids establish their capital in Baghdad.

969 Fatimids conquer Egypt and establish the city of Cairo.

970 Seljuk Turks occupy Persia.

973 The Al-Azhar University is founded at Cairo.

1055 Seljuks seize Baghdad.

1096 The first crusade to the Holy Land begins.

1099 The Crusaders take Jerusalem.

1187 Salah al Din re-takes Jerusalem for the Muslims.

1258 Baghdad is destroyed by the Mongols.

1260 The Mamelukes take control of Egypt and Syria.

1453 The Ottomans capture Constantinople and make it their capital.

1517 The Ottomans conquer Egypt and Syria. Ottoman rule is established throughout the Middle East.

1798 France invades Egypt.

1801 France withdraws from Egypt.

1804–48 Mohammed Ali rules in Egypt.

1869 The Suez Canal opens.

1882 Popular uprising in Egypt, followed by British invasion and occupation.

1886 The American University of Beirut is founded.

1916 Hussein, Sherif of Mecca declares Arab independence. France and Britain draw up the Sykes-Picot agreement dividing the region into spheres of influence under their command.

1917 Britain signs the Balfour declaration in support of a Jewish state in Palestine.

1918–19 First Egyptian revolt against the British occupation led by Saad Zaghloul.

1920 The British Mandate is established in Palestine.

1921 Feisal, the son of Hussein of Mecca, is declared king of Iraq.

1922 British agree to recognize Egypt as a sovereign state. Sultan Fuad is crowned King.

1923 The state of Transjordan is created.

1925 The first National State University is founded in Cairo. The Qajar dynasty in Iran is overthrown in a coup led by Reza Khan.

1926 Ibn Saud challenges Hussein, Sherif of Mecca, and seizes control.

1932 Iraq is declared an independent state.

1936 An Anglo-Egyptian treaty is signed, officially ending the British occupation of Egypt, though British forces remain.

1936–38 Arabs revolt against British occupation in Palestine.

1939–45 Truce in Palestine.

1941 Reza Khan is deposed by Anglo-Soviet intervention in Iran. His son Mohammed Reza is put on the throne. France declares Lebanon a sovereign state.

1943 Independence is declared in Syria.

1946 Syrian independence is established. Abdallah, son of Hussein of Mecca, becomes king of Transjordan.

1947 The British end their mandate in Palestine and the UN votes for the partition of the country.

1948 The first Arab–Israeli war. The state of Israel is established.

1952 A successful coup d'état by young army officers in Egypt forces the abdication and exile of King Farouk.

1953 Egypt is declared a republic.

1954 Gamal Abdul Nasser takes control of power in Egypt.

1956 Egypt seizes control of the Suez Canal. The second Arab–Israeli war breaks out when Israel invades Egypt with British and French backing.

1958 Civil war in Lebanon. Coup d'état in Iraq ends monarchy.

1961 Iraq becomes the first country to nationalize its oil industry. Kuwait establishes independence.

1962 Yemen Arab Republic establishes independence.

1964 The first Palestinian National Council takes place in Jerusalem; the Palestine Liberation Organization is established.

1967 Third Arab–Israeli war, the 'June' or 'Six Day' war. Yemen People's Democratic Republic (South Yemen) is established as an independent state.

1968 A second coup in Iraq brings a Baathist regime to power.

1970 Sultan Qaboos of Oman deposes his father and takes control of the country. Civil war breaks out in Jordan with the forces of King Hussein fighting the Palestinians.

1971 The Federation of the United Arab Emirates is formed by seven small Gulf sheikhdoms. Qatar and Bahrain achieve independence.

1973 The fourth Arab-Israeli war breaks out, known as the 'Ramadan' or 'Yom Kippur' war. The Arabs employ the oil weapon for the first time.

1974 Yassir Arafat addresses the UN in New York on the Palestinian cause.

1975 Civil war breaks out in Lebanon. Suez Canal reopens.

1977 President Sadat of Egypt visits Israel in a peace initiative.

1978 Egypt and Israel sign the Camp David peace treaty.

1979 The Shah of Iran flees his country into exile and the Islamic republic under the leadership of Ayatollah Khomeini is established.

1980 The first president of Iran, Abol Hassan Bani-Sadr is elected, followed by the first parliament.

Index

Numbers in *italic* refer to captions and illustrations

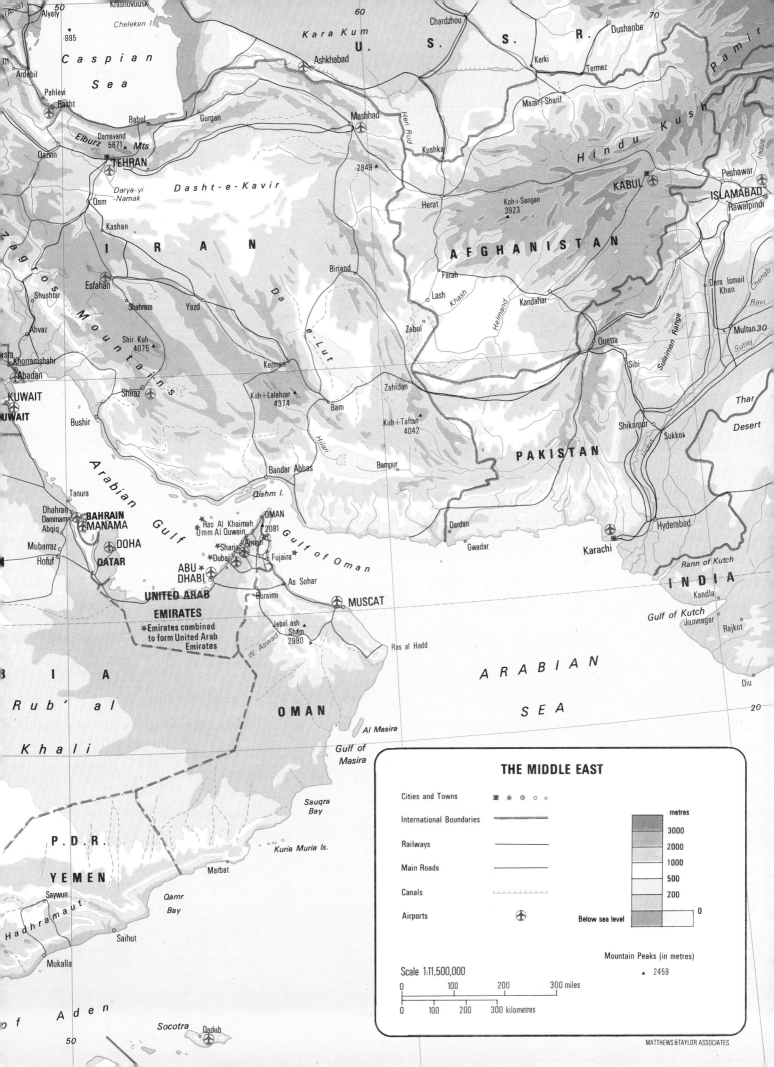

1 2 3 4 5 6 7 8 9 10—IL—88 87 86 85 84 83 82 81